Royal Navy
HANDBOOK

Martin H. Brice

LONDON

IAN ALLAN LTD

Cover; Invincible

First published 1985

ISBN 0 7110 1520 1

All rights reserved. No part of this book may be
reproduced or transmitted in any form or by any
means, electronic or mechanical, including photo-
copying, recording or by any information storage and
retrieval system, without permission from the
Publisher in writing.

© Martin H. Brice 1985

Published by Ian Allan Ltd, Shepperton, Surrey;
and printed by Ian Allan Printing Ltd at its works
at Coombelands in Runnymede, England

Contents

Left:
**HMS *Beaver* and her Westland Lynx
Helicopter.**

Acknowledgements

For providing photographs, material and information, making research facilities available, assisting on my photographic expeditions, checking and commenting on the typescript, and generally helping with advice and encouragement, I am particularly grateful to the following individuals and organisations: Airborne Forces Museum, Aldershot; Alton Area Library; Lt-Cdr C. P. Annis; P. G. W. Annis; Antigua & Barbuda Tourist Office; Vice-Adm Sir Patrick Bayly; HMS *Belfast*; John M. Bingeman; Second Officer A. C. Blackburn; Dr Alan Borg; Sylvia Brice; Buckler's Hard; Dan Chadwick; Captain Cook Museum, Middlesbrough; HMS *Cavalier*; Chicheley Hall, Newport Pagnell; Cleveland County Council; Cdr Richard Compton-Hall; Cornwall Aero Park & Flambards Village, Culdrose; Denise Cutts; A. Denholm; Duxford Airfield (Imperial War Museum), Cambridgeshire; Borough of Eastbourne Tourism & Leisure Department; Farnborough Reference Library; Andrew Farrow; R. J. Fisher; T. H. Fitch; Simon Forty; HMS *Fearless*; The *Foudroyant* Trust; Gordon Frater; HMS *Gannet* (1878) Society; Maurice Gardener; S. W. Hackman; J. K. Hale; G. Hales; Charles W. Hawkins; Andrew Holme; Capt M. A. Hemmings; A. J. Holland; Imperial War Museum, London; The *Invincible* (1758) Committee; Irene Kentsbeer; Michael Lennon; Loughton Reference Library; The Maritime Trust; Colin J. Marsden; The *Mary Rose* Trust; John Maulkin; Dennis Mayne; Tony Merriman; Michael J. Mitchell; Monmouth District Council; S. Mower; David S. Muffett; National Maritime Museum, Greenwich; National War Museum, Malta; Naval Ordnance Museum, Gosport; Orkney Natural History Museum, Stromness; C. T. Parsons; Capt R. H. Parsons; City of Portsmouth Directorate of Leisure & Tourism; Cdr Peter Reynolds; Dr Ray Riley; J. N. Robertson; Arthur Rogers; Royal Marines Museum, Eastney; Royal Naval Air Station, Yeovilton; Royal Naval Hospital, Haslar; Royal Naval Museum, Portsmouth; Royal Navy Submarine Museum, Gosport; Cdr L. M. M. Saunders Watson; Scottish United Services Museum, Edinburgh; Ship's Preservation Trust Ltd, Hartlepool; Roy Smith; Southampton Central Reference Library; W. Roderick Stewart; Jack W. Sweet; *Unicorn* Preservation Society, Dundee; Althea van der Poole; Philip Vella; HMS *Victory*; Sheila Watson; Col K. M. Wilkins; B. S. Wilson; Edward A. Wilson; Stephen Wood; the 102 Trust. Those photographs taken especially for this book were developed and printed by Fisher Photographic of Alton and Basingstoke. All photos are courtesy MoD unless otherwise credited.

Other books by the author

Landing Craft (Outline Publications)
Stronghold (Batsford)
M-Class Submarines (Outline Publications)
Axis Blockade Runners of World War II (Batsford)
The Royal Navy During The Sino-Japanese Incident 1937-1941 (Ian Allan)
The Royal Navy — A Young Person's Guide (MacMillan)
The Tribals (Ian Allan)

with C. W. Hawkins
Alton: A Pictorial Biography (Local Heritage Books)

with Keiren Phelan
Fast Attack Craft (Macdonald & Jane's)

Author's Notice

I have visited nearly all the publicly accessible places described in this book, and in other instances, I have corresponded with the appropriate authorities. It should be recognised that all the information contained herein is that available at the time of research. This is especially true in the case of admission fees. The reader ought to assume that those quoted are the *minimum* and that any alteration since the preparation of this book will be an *increase* — and that includes the possibility of introducing charges at places where admission was originally quoted as free. I shall be pleased to hear from any reader or from any of the organisations mentioned in this work regarding updated amendments for possible future editions of this book.

I have only mentioned the nearest railway station if it provides easy access to the place being described. A car or taxi journey of several miles after leaving the train does not constitute easy access.

Bus services are not mentioned. They can be erratic, especially in country areas where certain routes may only run on certain days of the week. A lengthy list of bus numbers passing the entrance can thus give a misleading impression of accessibility.

Car parking facilities are not mentioned unless part of the place being described.

Facilities for the disabled are only mentioned if the authorities responsible make it very clear that they can be accommodated.

Refreshment facilities can vary considerably — in accessibility and menu, often according to the season — while some places provide picnic areas. Like so many individual items in this book, the single topic of refreshments could fill an entire volume on its own; and as this is a handbook to the Royal Navy and not a good food guide, no mention has been made about refreshments.

Finally, a note about the length of time it takes to go round a museum or preserved ship. I find that this depends on *me*, rather than the place. A hurried walk-round in the last 30min before closing-time can sometimes convey an impression, highlight one particular exhibit of significant memory, which would have been totally submerged by a welter of images if I had spent the whole day there. On the other hand, I have passed four hours just looking at the displays, quite apart from time taken over meals or at the salestall. One winter I spent every Saturday afternoon at the National Maritime Museum, never trying to look at more than one gallery at a visit. With the introduction of charges and their inevitable increase, such a pastime would be very costly, but the enthusiast for one particular museum would be well advised to join its Friends' society or enquire about some other form of season ticket. Some national organisations also have season tickets, admitting the holder to a range of museums, galleries and other sites under their control or with which they are associated.

There does remain the problem of queues, especially at peak periods, at the more popular sites with restricted viewing facilties. Whether to stay or go, must be your decision, largely depending on how likely you are to visit that area again. But it is worth remembering that well-publicised, temporary exhibitions are not always the only chance you have of seeing that material. Often when the special exhibition closes, many of its items are eventually returned to their proper place in adjoining galleries, where they can later be seen in comfortable leisure instead of in a crowded gallery. Of course, events like air displays, pageants and *son et lumière* presentations, can only be witnessed on the day they actually occur.

This book is intended to be carried in the car, pocket or bag. If you happen to be in the area of some place it describes and therefore decide to visit it as a result of what you read, it is worth risking disappointment. But if you are planning a special trip to see something in particular, especially if you are taking a party of people, then contact the place first to confirm opening times, admission fees (there may be concessions for party bookings), and everything else you need to know. (Certainly, it should be assumed that reference departments may only be visited by prior appointment.) Make what arrangements *you* think are necessary regarding refreshments, etc. But always leave something to chance. Be prepared to change your plans to accommodate some new sight or event.

For, if your little outing contains the ingredients of forward planning, good navigation and a spirit of adventure, you will already be following in some of the traditions of the Royal Navy.

Introduction to the Royal Navy

'It is upon the navy under the Providence of God that the safety, honour and welfare of this realm do chiefly depend.'

There is no reason to assume that those words of Charles II, penned as *Preamble* to the *Articles of War*, represent an outdated concept. In spite of high-speed means of travel, complex networks of international trade and alliance, and long-range destructive weaponry, Britain remains an island. No friendly visitor, no hostile invader, no vital commodity, can enter the United Kingdom except by crossing the sea. Nor can any carefree tourist, dedicated salesman or manufactured product leave the United Kingdom except by crossing the sea. Most may travel by air or send invisible electronic messages, but all must traverse the water, even though it may only be the Straits of Dover. If that traffic is interrupted, the nation's life is inevitably dislocated.

Most at risk are the nation's supplies of food and energy, and its ability to conduct foreign policy — itself an indirect method of safeguarding those same supplies of food and energy as well as preventing hostile invasion. There is no doubt that British farms produce a greater proportion of the nation's food than earlier this century, but they still do not grow *all* the food the people eat. And even that production is only accomplished with considerable reliance upon imported fuels, fertilisers, animal feedstuffs and equipment. As regards the nation's energy supplies, the very name of North Sea oil indicates its delivery by surface tanker or undersea pipeline. Meanwhile satellites may seem to provide foolproof global communications; but their signals can be intercepted and they themselves cannot be concealed in the same way as cables laid along the seabed.

It is the Royal Navy's function to protect all this maritime traffic according to current strategic, tactical and technical doctrine. Another role is the forwarding of national policy, either in co-operation with allies, or by showing the flag in foreign ports (for who can tell whether today's non-aligned country will be tomorrow's friend or enemy?); or — if it is necessary for troops to be deployed — by screening their movement and providing an offshore base for them. The Falklands campaign is the most obvious example of the last-named responsibility, but there have been several such operations since 1945.

These traditional tasks have not been eliminated by the danger of atomic warfare. Indeed, the Royal Navy's own contribution to the mutual deterrence of nuclear confrontation has its parallels in history. The line-of-battle-ships of the Age of Sail fought few full-scale engagements. They 'held the ring', while most action was seen by frigates and sloops convoying transports on some amphibious assault, or beating off attacks by commerce-raiding privateers. Then later, in each of two world wars this century, there was only one stand-up fight between rival lines of dreadnoughts. For most of their existence these mighty arbiters of early 20th century seapower 'held the ring', while submarine and escort, aircraft and carrier, mine and sweep, landing craft and shore battery, decided the outcome of the conflict at sea. Similarly, the Royal Navy's Polaris submarines are the capital ships of the nuclear age. It is not inconceivable that in some future emergency, they — together with all the other nuclear deterrent forces — might 'hold the ring', while the war itself is fought with missile-armed and electronically-shielded, but otherwise conventional, units.

This has been the situation in every conflict since 1945. Indeed, before both world wars it was confidently forecast that their opening stages would be marked by massive naval or aerial bombardment of the British Isles. In fact, in both those wars it was maritime blockade and global attrition which came nearest to defeating the British people. Those responsible for planning the defence of the United Kingdom cannot disregard the possibility of such a situation being repeated.

Yet, in spite of the continued importance of the Royal Navy to Britain's well-being, and in spite of the popularity of maritime programmes on the television, the general public is probably less familiar with the Navy than with other services. Every day people see aeroplanes overhead; they themselves travel in airliners, there is a flying display somewhere every summer weekend. Meanwhile, motorists pass columns of army trucks and tank transporters along the highway; tourists take photographs of colourful uniforms outside royal palaces; and, in less happier circumstances, some people have become used to encountering soldiers aiding the civil authorities in enforcing law and order.

But the Royal Navy is rarely seen except in port, its ships undergoing repair, its personnel coming ashore on leave or on some training course. Occasionally there is the drama of a rescue at sea, but usually the only public indication is the sight of survivors being landed, now largely recovered from their ordeal. Admittedly there are Navy Days, but their displays and drills and blank-firings can only demonstrate how the equipment works. They can only hint at the broader issues of maritime strategy, which can often be considered effective when nothing unusual appears to be happening.

For it is then that the tankers, freighters and troopships are proceeding on their way, while a distant screen or close escort of warships and aircraft continually scans the sky, probes the depths or sweeps the seabed, for hostile attacker or explosive device. And of course, in peacetime, such activity must of happy necessity be for exercise only.

This book is therefore intended as a general guide to the modern Royal Navy, an explanation of what it is, what it does, where it can be seen, and its place in history. It is divided into five sections:

1   Where to see the Royal Navy.
2   The Ships and Aircraft of the Royal Navy.
3   The Organisation of the Royal Navy.
4   The Historic Royal Navy.
5   The Hidden Royal Navy.

The titles of **sections 1** and **2** are self-explanatory. **Section 3** outlines the

Above left:
A Westland Lynx helicopter over the Type 42 destroyer HMS *Birmingham*.

Above:
The Portsmouth Division Royal Naval Memorial on Southsea Common.
Author

Left:
The frigate HMS *Brazen* (Type 22 — left) and HMS *Rothesay* (Type 12 — right) fuelling from RFA *Blue Rover* in the Indian Ocean.

Below:
The Type 42 destroyer HMS *Southampton* leaving Portsmouth.

command structure of the Fleet, and explains the relationship between the Navy and its reserves and auxiliary units. **Section 4** is a chronological listing of those preserved ships and naval museums which together portray the complete history of the Royal Navy from the reign of Henry VIII to the present day. It can be reasonably argued that the maritime interest of both nation and monarch can be traced back to a much earlier date. During the Middle Ages, the Cinque Ports provided ships of war for the king. Before then, there were the maritime activities of Alfred the Great. Even earlier than that, the Count of the Saxon Shore maintained a Roman 'Grand Fleet' in British waters. But the Cinque Ports' vessels were temporarily-converted merchantmen, a private-enterprise navy in every sense. Nor do the earlier organisations represent the establishment of a permanent state-owned force of purpose-built warships and full-time personnel which could be regarded as the genuine beginning of the Royal Navy as we know it. For that we must look to the Tudor period.

Section 5 does not refer to those aspects of the Royal Navy which have to be kept hidden for reasons of national security. Nevertheless, this is a good place to mention such matters. Ever since the Navy began in the Tudor period, its security has been a sensitive issue. At a time when soldiers were customarily billeted in private dwellings and ale-houses, warships and their crews were berthed behind high dockyard walls or moored in inaccessible creeks. This was partly to hinder pilfering and desertion, but it also prevented hostile agents fomenting disaffection and wrecking installations and equipment. (Hanging as punishment for murder was abolished in 1965, but was retained for setting fire to, and for other malicious damage in, HM Dockyards if this is done with treasonable intent — an indication of the importance of such installations to the state.)

Being thus largely isolated from the rest of British society and even from the other armed forces, the Royal Navy developed the tradition of going about its business without making a fuss, and if possible, without saying anything about its work. It was 'The Silent Service', an appellation it has retained even in the publicity-concious 20th century.

So, bear in mind the Royal Navy's reputation for reticence and security. Do not abuse the Navy's hospitality. If the notice says 'No Admittance' or 'No Cameras', it means exactly that. If in doubt ASK! And even if you are not in doubt, still ASK just the same — it is courteous to do so and it sets people's minds at rest. And if the answer is 'No', it may be disappointing but it still means NO!

Having covered that matter, it can now be explained that the purpose of **section 5 — The Hidden Royal Navy**, is to remind the reader of how much the Royal Navy has influenced the things we see around us every day, no matter how far we live from the coast. To attempt a definitive listing of all such items is obviously impossible. By the very nature of its material, this section cannot help but be imprecise and open-ended. But I hope that the reader may be prompted to undertake his or her own local research; perhaps noting advertisements with maritime themes; photographing the signs of inns named after admirals; or finding out streets named after naval battles. After all, Samuel Pepys enjoyed copying out lists of names of ships. Certainly, the present author's own youthful interest in the Navy was accelerated by such a pastime. Who knows where your project may eventually take you?

Where to see the Royal Navy

The headquarters of the Royal Navy is situated in London and has always been very near the seat of government. Henry VIII's Navy Board of administrative civil servants was located on Tower Hill adjoining the Tower of London. Its offices have long since disappeared, its functions being transferred to other buildings and departments.

The first Admiralty Office to house the politically-appointed and professional-seagoing directorate of the Navy was built near the royal palace of Whitehall in 1693-94, the main construction being completed in 1722-26. It served as a block of apartments where the Lords Commissioner for the execution of the Office of Lord High Admiral, could reside while conducting state business in the Palace of Whitehall. The only room which could be termed a real 'office' was the Board Room, where the Lords of the Admiralty could meet in conference. The entrance portico known as Admiralty Screen was erected by Robert Adam in 1759-61. The First Sea Lord was given his own private residence (Admiralty House — only accessible from within the Admiralty Office) in 1786-88. Further extensions followed at the rear of the complex in 1894-95.

By now the Admiralty had also become the Navy's strategic headquarters, orders sent by mechanical and electric telegraphs deploying fleets all around the world. The development of wireless-telegraphy and radio-telephony speeded up such communications and on occasions enabled the Admiralty to exercise tactical control over distant maritime operations.

The massive citadel at the back of the Admiralty was built in World War 2 to house plotting rooms and communications centres, which were manned day and night. Some signals were despatched and received via aerials on the roof of the Admiralty, but most were sent by landline to powerful transmitters which then beamed the coded instructions to ships at sea. *(Nearest station: Charing Cross.)*

The Board of Admiralty was absorbed into the unified Ministry of Defence in 1964. Since then the Old Admiralty Building has lost some of its former significance. A number of its administrative and policymaking functions have been transferred to the Ministry of Defence Main Building farther down Whitehall. Many routine tasks are undertaken in the Empress State Building, a high tower block in Lillie Road, Fulham SW6 1TR. Its departments include the Naval Historical Branch and the Naval Historical Reference Library, open by appointment to students of maritime affairs. *(Tel: (01)-835 1244. Nearest stations: West Brompton and Earl's Court.)*

Besides offices, the London area is the location of a number of depots and other establishments providing services and facilities not only in London but for the Navy as a whole. There is a Royal Naval Stores Depot at Deptford, the Admiralty Research Laboratory at Teddington, the Admiralty Engineering Laboratory at West Drayton, the Admiralty Oil Laboratory at Cobham, and the Admiralty Compass Laboratory at Slough. Members of the Women's Royal Naval Service working in London are based at Furse House in Queen's Gate Terrace, HMS *St Vincent*, while Naval policing in London is undertaken by the Royal Naval Patrol based in Iverna Gardens.

The control of maritime operations is now conducted from Eastbury Park, Norwood, Middlesex, where the headquarters of RAF Allied Maritime Air Force Channel and Eastern Atlantic is also situated. (Similar RAF headquarters of what used to be known as 'Coastal Command' are located in other appropriate RN and NATO shore establishments, ensuring the closest air-sea co-operation.)

Eastbury Park is officially designated HMS *Warrior*, for in the Royal Navy a shore establishment is commissioned as one of Her Majesty's Ships. Thus officers and ratings assigned duty at any of the offices or depots in London are recorded as being appointed to HMS *St Vincent*. This title has now replaced the old name HMS *President* as the Royal Navy's generic term for the Admiralty and Ministry of Defence. The name HMS *President* is now reserved for the actual ship — a sloop of 1918. Berthed alongside the north bank of the River Thames between Blackfriars and Waterloo Bridges, *President* and her sister-ship *Chrysanthemum* serve as headquarters drill-ships for the London Division of the Royal Naval Reserve and the Women's Royal Naval Reserve. Minesweepers and other coastal craft sometimes come upriver to these vessels, thus providing practical experience for reserve personnel under training. *(Nearest stations: Temple and Blackfriars.)*

Larger warships on official visits to the nation's capital can berth outboard of the preserved HMS *Belfast* in the Pool of London. Good vantage points to see such vessels are the riverside walk in front of the Tower of London, Tower Bridge, and HMS *Belfast* herself (the usual admission charge applying). Sometimes visiting warships are open to the public. Details can be obtained from HMS *Belfast (Tel: (01)-407 6434)* or from the Naval Liaison Officer, London *(Tel: (01)-218 2295)*. Of course, operational requirements can easily result in changes of plan and curtailment of previously-quoted times of opening. *(Nearest stations: Tower Hill and London Bridge.)*

Farther downstream is Greenwich where very large visiting warships sometimes anchor opposite the Royal Naval College. On such occasions they can be seen either from Greenwich Pier (near the *Cutty Sark*) or from Island Gardens on the Isle of Dogs. Pedestrians can cross from Greenwich to the north bank of the river via a tunnel.

The Royal Naval College, Greenwich is for sub-lieutenants and other junior officers undertaking detailed study of the theory of their profession. There are also staff courses for captains and other senior officers. The Royal Naval College, Greenwich, is in effect the University of the Royal Navy. It is housed in the Royal Hospital, founded by Queen Mary (Consort of William III) in 1694. Originally designed by Sir Christopher Wren, it was intended to accommodate disabled seamen, educate their orphans and promote the study of navigation. Completed in 1752, the Hospital could eventually house some 2,170 Pensioners, while additional buildings catered for the establishment's other chartered responsibilities. On formal occasions, Pensioners assembled in the Painted Hall, its walls and ceilings covered with majestic allegorical paintings by Sir James Thornhill. Nelson's body lay in state here before being conveyed by barge to St Paul's Cathedral. Due to the development of other forms of social welfare, the Hospital was closed in 1869 and four years later it became the Royal Naval College.

The Painted Hall and Chapel of the Royal Naval College are open to the public from 2.30 to 5pm every day except Thursdays, when the Hall is being prepared for Officers' Guest Night dinner. It is also closed on Good Fridays and if it is being used for other official functions; and in common with most government monuments, is closed on Christmas Eve, Christmas Day, Boxing Day and New Year's Day. Admission is free. *(Tel: (01)-858 2154. Nearest stations: Maze Hill and Greenwich. Also: boat trips from Westminster and Charing Cross.)*

Portsmouth

During the Royal Navy's history, a number of places have served as the Fleet's main base, according to the demands of international politics and technical advance. Portsmouth has long been of major significance to Britain's maritime development. King John ordered a dock to be laid out there in 1212, on an even earlier site. However, located where HMS *Vernon* now fronts the harbour, it was merely a shelving strand on which ships could be beached, drying out at low tide to be surrounded by a temporary earth rampart. The world's first purpose-built dry dock, which could be separated from the sea and emptied or filled as required, was not opened until 1495-96, and that too was at Portsmouth. Its sides were of wood and in the next reign it became the centrepiece of a growing complex of facilities for ship construction, repair and maintenance, all defended by fortifications, and all part of Henry VIII's appreciation of the Navy as an instrument of national policy.

Successive centuries saw the expansion of the dockyard, especially after the Industrial Revolution. This not only resulted in the construction of steam-driven ironclads, but was also reflected in the architecture of the dockyard — 18th and 19th century buildings of brick and iron housing mass-production machinery. Some historic buildings (such as Boat Houses Nos 5 and 7 over the former Mast Pond) can be seen by visitors en route to HMS *Victory*. Others (such as Sir Samuel Bentham's block mills of 1800, which accommodated Marc Isambard Brunel's blockmaking machinery for the 'Wooden Walls of England') are in parts of the dockyard not accessible to the public.

For Portsmouth is not merely a living museum, but an integral part of the modern defences of the realm. This is shown by the following list of present-day Naval establishments in and around Portsmouth Dockyard.

HMS *Nelson*

This is the generic term for the Royal Navy Base and Barracks, Portsmouth, where personnel are accommodated while awaiting posting to a seagoing warship. It includes the Royal Naval School of Educational & Training Technology, the Royal Naval Dental Training School, and the Royal Naval Detention Quarters. In addition, HMS *Nelson* is the flagship of two admirals:

● The Flag Officer Third Flotilla/NATO Anti-Submarine Group Two (although the operational control of this force is conducted from Fort Southwick on Portsdown).

● The Flag Officer Portsmouth, responsible for the dockyard itself (which is the main base of the Royal Navy's seagoing fleet and contains everything for refitting, repairing and building warships); for Portsmouth Harbour and its approaches (the maintenance of buoys and channels and their defences, etc); and for the Fleet Technical Staff. The fact that Portsmouth — indeed, all the Royal Dockyards — are being privatised or managed on commercial principles, should not lessen their importance to the State, nor should it alter their function as repair and stores bases for the Fleet. It does mean however, that more warships may be refitted at other ports, thus increasing the opportunities for seeing them away from their customary bases; conversely, the 'Royal' dockyards should now be able to refit merchant ships.

(Public Navy Days in late August; Tel: (0705) 822351, ext 23430.)

HMS *Victory*

Permanently preserved in dry dock, the *Victory* is also the flagship of Naval Home Command, the admiral responsible for personnel, ships and establishments in and around the British Isles.

HMS *Vernon*

To the south of the main dockyard is the establishment which comprises the Royal Naval Seamanship School, the Minewarfare School, the Diving School, the Headquarters for Mine Counter-Measures Vessels (MCMV) Support, the Fleet Clearance Headquarters, and the base for the 2nd MCM Squadron and for the Portsmouth and Medway Clearance Diving Teams. *Vernon* has been the traditional name for the Navy's torpedo and mine establishment since 1872. *(Public Searchlight Tattoo in mid-September; Tel: (0705) 822351 ext 2522.)*

HMS *Temeraire*

The Royal Navy's School of Physical Training in Flathouse Road, Portsmouth.

HMS *Excellent*

HMS *Excellent* has long had the reputation of setting the standard for the Royal Navy's drill and discipline. It is located to the north of the dockyard, on Whale Island, which was largely formed of spoil dredged from 19th century dockyard extensions. Originally the Royal Navy's Gunnery School, it now comprises the following Schools: Naval Gunnery Training; Nuclear, Bacteriological and Chemical Defence; Divisional and Management; Regulating (ie, Police); Advanced Photography; Leading Rates Leadership; and Internal Security.

In addition, HMS *Excellent* is the headquarters of the Experimental and Trials Department and the base for Weapons Trials. *(Public Field Gun Displays in June; Tel (0705) 826722 Portsmouth Information Centre.)*

Eastney

The headquarters of the Royal Marines' Training Group on the southeast corner of Portsea Island.

More naval establishments are located on the Gosport side of Portsmouth Harbour.

HMS *Dolphin* '

Sometimes known as Fort Blockhouse after the building where it is accommodated, this is the base of the 1st Submarine Squadron and the Submarine School; look for a tall, square, white tower — it is filled with water and is the Submarine Escape Training Tank. *(Public Open Day in late July; Tel (07017) 29217.)*

Royal Clarence Victualling Yard

Formally established as the headquarters of the Royal Navy's Victualling Department in 1828, on the site of an existing depot for issuing food to warships. The buildings include a flour mill and bakery for making ship's biscuit. It is just to the north of the Gosport Ferry and is now a stores issuing depot with its own jetties.

The Royal Naval Hospital, Haslar

Built in 1746-62, this is the only existing establishment of its kind in the Navy; other bases have 'sick quarters'.

Admiralty Marine Engineering Establishment, Haslar

Concerned with propulsion machinery in warships.

Admiralty Experiment Works, Haslar

Founded in Torquay in 1872 by William Froude, the AEW moved to Haslar in 1886. Its buildings include huge tanks in which models of future warships and full-sized equipment (such as propellers and periscopes) can be tested in a variety of sea conditions.

Royal Naval Armament Depot, Gosport

Concerned with the storage and issue of ammunition and ordnance of practically every type. Originally established at Priddy's Hard, it has expanded to include Frater and Bedenham, covering virtually the whole of the shoreline of Portsmouth Harbour from Gosport to Fareham.

Royal Naval Aircraft Yard, Fleetlands

The largest helicopter maintenance facility in Europe.

HMS *Centurion*

The Naval Drafting Headquarters in Grange Road, responsible for allocating personnel to ships and establishments throughout the world.

Fort Rowner

A 19th century Army fort for the defence of the land approaches to Portsmouth Harbour. It is now the headquarters of the Royal Navy's degaussing organisation. It ensures that British warships and merchantmen are provided with equipment which reverses the vessel's polarity or otherwise alters its magnetic signature, thus making it less likely to detonate magnetic mines.

HMS *Sultan*
The Royal Naval Marine Engineering School.

HMS *Daedalus*
One of the earliest Royal Naval Air Stations to be established, at Lee-on-Solent. The airfield and its environs house the following: Royal Naval Air Engineering School; Naval Air Technical Evaluation Centre; Naval Air Trial Installation Unit; Accident Investigation Unit; Mobile Aircraft Repair, Transport and Salvage Unit; Naval Aircraft Aircrew and Marine Examination Board; Naval Aircrew Advisory Board; Air Medical School; Central Air Medical Board; Survival and Equipment School; Royal Naval Establishment, Seafield Park.

The duties of helicopters at *Daedalus* (and indeed at any other RNAS) include Search and Rescue in co-operation with the Royal National Lifeboat Institution and the Coastguards. *(Public Open Day in mid-July; Tel (0705) 826722.)*

HMS *Collingwood*
Situated between Fareham and Gosport, this is the Royal Navy's Weapon & Electrical Engineering School. It includes the Digital Systems School for computer training.

Portsdown
Up on Portsdown, to the north of Portsmouth Harbour are the Admiralty Surface Weapons Establishment and the Admiralty Compass Laboratory. Its buildings are surmounted by a variety of aerials and lattice masts.

HMS *Dryad*
Also located on Portsdown — in Fort Southwick — this is the Headquarters of the Flag Officer Third Flotilla/NATO Anti-Submarine Group Two. In addition it accommodates the School of Maritime Operations and the Maritime Tactical School. Fort Southwick is a 19th century Army fort (one of 'Palmerston's Follies' built for the landward defence of Portsmouth against French invasion). *Dryad's* wardroom is actually located some distance away in Southwick House, formerly the Headquarters for the Allied invasion of Normandy. The Naval Wall Map in the wardroom has been preserved in the situation it displayed at H-Hour on D-Day, 6 June 1944. It can sometimes be seen on prior application by letter to the Command Officer, HMS *Dryad*.

HMS *Mercury*
This is the Communication and Navigation Faculty of the School of Maritime Operations and is located near Butser Hill between Portsmouth and Petersfield.

Royal Naval Stores Depot, Woolston
Near Southampton.

Vantage Points
Virtually anywhere on Portsea Island from Southsea Castle to the Gosport Ferry is a good vantage point, while on the Gosport side, there are the Ferry

Above:
Usually all that people can see of the Royal Navy's activities is a distant warship on the far horizon (HMS *Lowestoft* off Lowestoft, 23 July 1984) . . .

Below:
. . . or a quick glimpse of Fleet Air Arm aircraft returning to base (Westland Lynx helicopters landing at HMS *Daedalus*, Lee-on-Solent, 8 August 1984). . . .

Bottom:
. . . But far out at sea, the Royal Navy is at work. A Westland Sea King helicopter from 819 Squadron takes divers of the Royal Navy's Scotland & Northern Ireland Explosive Ordnance Disposal Team to inspect North Sea gas production platforms after a warning that bombs might have been planted on them. *Author/MoD*

Above:

The nuclear-powered fleet submarine HMS *Trafalgar* passing HMS *Illustrious* in 1983. The aircraft carrier is leaving Plymouth after being open to the public during a weekend of Navy Days.

Below:

The Type 21 frigate HMS *Amazon* keeps watch on a Soviet 'Kildin' class destroyer towing a support tanker past the Channel Islands. Personnel on the British bridge still find time to wave to the cameraman.

Above:

A Sea King helicopter from 820 Squadron 'dunks' a sonar listening device into the North Atlantic as a Russian 'Foxtrot' class submarine passes in the background.

Top:
**V/STOL aircraft carriers of the 1980s:
HMS** *Illustrious* **and the Russian**
Novorossiysk.

Above:
**The Royal Navy must be ready for
action at any time and in any part of
the world. Less than a year after this
tranquil scene was photographed at
Devonport Dockyard, the Type 21
frigate HMS** *Antelope* **had been sunk
during the Falklands War. Note the
'Ham' class inshore minesweeper
ahead of her.** *Colin J. Marsden*

Left:
A Sun-Company tug guides HMS *Osiris*
**into the Pool of London to berth
alongside HMS** *Belfast*, **on 26 April
1984.**

Pier Gardens, Rampart Walk and publicly accessible roads round to Gilkicker. Being the base of the Third Flotilla/NATO Anti-Submarine Group Two (which includes assault ships and 'Invincible' class carriers), means that it is possible to see those vessels of that force which are not currently serving off the Falklands. When leaving or entering Portsmouth for or after a day's exercises in the Channel, they are often accompanied by a frigate squadron.

However, nearly every ship of the Royal Navy comes to Portsmouth at some stage in its career. There are also 'O' class submarines and minecraft proceeding to HMS *Dolphin* and *Vernon* respectively, plus Royal Fleet Auxiliary vessels bound to and from the Royal Clearance Victualling Yard. In addition Portsmouth, like all other British ports, can be visited by NATO warships and by other navies' vessels.

Portchester Castle (itself a Roman naval base almost 2,000 years old) is a good place for viewing ships moored in Fareham Creek while awaiting disposal and scrapping (sometimes known as 'Death Row'). From time to time, some of these vessels may be used as stationary training ships to provide practical experience for personnel on courses in *Sultan* and *Collingwood*.

Vessels for disposal are usually moored very close together and may have already had some pieces of equipment removed; their pennant numbers may be obscured or have deteriorated, so it is not always easy to identify them.

Close-up views of many of the ships in port can be obtained from 'trips round the harbour', which depart from Southsea and Gosport.

Royal Naval helicopters and hovercraft operating from HMS *Daedalus* can be seen from the shore at Lee-on-Solent. There is a slipway enabling hovercraft to reach the sea after crossing the main road which separates the RNAS from the beach. *Daedalus* frequently provides a temporary home for helicopters from warships visiting Portsmouth or undergoing refit there. *(The nearest railway stations in the area are Portsmouth Harbour, Portsmouth & Southsea, Fratton, Cosham, Portchester and Fareham.)*

Portland

Government interest in the Weymouth area as a defence against invasion dates from the reign of Henry VIII, who built Sandsfoot Castle (on the mainland at Wyke Regis) and Portland Castle (on the Isle itself). Their guns dominated the anchorage and protected friendly warships and merchantmen sheltering from southwesterly gales in the lee of the long strand of pebbles known as Chesil Beach. In the mid-19th century, a breakwater was constructed to screen the anchorage from heavy seas from the other direction. From then on Portland became the main operational base of the Channel Fleet, with considerable stocks of fuel — at first coal, and later oil. It was the site of the Whitehead torpedo factory and by 1939 was the home of HMS *Osprey*, the Navy's anti-submarine school.

Portland Harbour is where the only Royal Navy Victoria Cross to be won in home waters was earned by Acting Leading Seaman Jack Foreman Mantle on 4 July 1940. He kept firing his gun all through a dive-bombing attack, although the anti-aircraft ship he was in (HMS *Foylebank*) was hit and sinking. The award was a posthumous one.

Portland is still the home of HMS *Osprey*, but it is now the working-up

base for ships commissioning after construction or refit. It is the flagship of the Flag Officer, Sea Training, and its establishment includes RNAS Portland. This comprises the Royal Naval Air Anti-Submarine School and the Royal Naval Air Search and Rescue School. The squadrons of helicopters based there are: 829 (Westland Wasps for aircrew training); 815 and 702 (Westland Lynx for embarkation in seagoing ships and aircrew training respectively); and 772 (Westland Wessex Mk 5 for co-operation with the ships working up off Portland).
(Public Navy Days in mid-July; Tel (0305) 820311.)
The Admiralty Underwater Weapons Establishment built in 1948-52 is also on Portland, at Weston.

Vantage Points

Because Portland is primarily an open anchorage with limited berthing facilities, it is not usually possible to see the ships close-up — unless from a 'trip round the harbour' boat out of Weymouth. However, good general views of Portland Harbour can be obtained from Sandsfoot Castle Gardens (*nearest station: Weymouth*) and from the top of the northern escarpment on Portland itself.

One of the more unusual vessels to be seen is HMS *Crystal* — a dumb barge of skyscraper proportions used for underwater experiments.

Most Royal Navy warships come to Portland at some time to do their sea training and they can be seen from Portland Bill actually exercising in the Channel. On my last visit there, there were no less than seven warships in sight. Two of them were frigates practising fuelling at sea from an RFA oiler, and an assault ship was landing on helicopters while being screened by another frigate.

Dartmouth

The *Britannia* Royal Naval College was built in 1899-1905, overlooking Dartmouth. It replaced a collection of 'wooden walls' moored in the River Dart to accommodate cadets joining the Navy. The most important of these old vessels was HMS *Britannia*, and the College perpetuates its name. At first, new entrants were only 13 years old, but nowadays the young men and women preparing to be officers at the College are of more mature age, and many of them have already served several years as ratings in the Navy. Besides basic training and theoretical instruction, they gain practical experience by going to sea in warships allocated to that role. On such occasions these vessels can be seen in the Dart from both Dartmouth and Kingswear. *(Kingswear is the nearest station, but this is a preserved railway and not part of BR.)*

Plymouth

The story that Sir Francis Drake was playing bowls on Plymouth Hoe when he learned of the Armada's approach may be a mythical one, but it is a reminder that Plymouth was England's principal naval base during the wars with Spain. Like so much activity in the reign of Elizabeth I, many of those naval operations were a mixture of state direction and private enterprise. The early history of the dockyard at Plymouth reflects that combination. The defences of Sutton Pool and its approaches, included a fort of 1592, erected where Charles II's Citadel now stands. However, local shipbuilding and repairing facilities were privately owned until William III founded a royal dockyard in 1691. It was sited slightly to the west of Plymouth, on the shore of the Hamoaze (as that stretch of the River Tamar is called). Its expansion — with drydocks, mast houses, mast ponds, slipways, roperies, gun wharves, barracks, offices, admiral's house, stores, and hulks for free convict labour — paralleled similar developments at Portsmouth and Chatham. In 1824 Plymouth Dock became Devonport, the name by which it is known today. Meanwhile Plymouth Sound itself was being made a safer anchorage, thanks to the construction of the Breakwater.

Devonport's latest facility is the Submarine Refit Complex for the largest nuclear-powered boats. Opened by HRH The Prince of Wales on 23 May 1980, it includes two drydocks, and is dominated by a huge crane, 42m high.

Devonport is officially known in the Royal Navy as HMS *Drake* and is the flagship of the Flag Officer Plymouth. He is also NATO's COMPLYMCHAN and COMCENTLANT, responsible for the protection of maritime traffic in the central Atlantic and the Western Approaches to the English Channel. He therefore has directional command over anti-aircraft and anti-submarine frigates and minecraft, plus submarines for offensive action against hostile vessels. (The 2nd Submarine Squadron consists of nuclear-powered boats from the 'S', 'T', and 'Valiant' classes.) His Maritime Headquarters where he conducts operations are actually located at Mount Wise (between Devonport and Plymouth), the establishment being known as HMS *Vivid*.

The rest of HMS *Drake* comprises: the Royal Naval Barracks; the Signal Training Centre; the Royal Naval School of Hydrographic Surveying; the Royal Naval Diving Centre & Plymouth Clearance Diving Team; the Naval Provost Marshal; and the provision of Naval Liaison Officers for the Merchant Navy.

Like every naval base, HMS *Drake* also includes local Leadership, Firefighting and Seamanship Schools. *(Public Navy Days in late August; Tel (0752) 555914/5.)*

Other Royal Navy establishments in the area are:

HMS *Defiance*
The Fleet Maintenance Base located within the Dockyard.

HMS *Raleigh*
At Torpoint in Cornwall, on the opposite bank of the Hamoaze. It is the Royal Naval New Entry Training Establishment, where newly-joined ratings receive their basic training and introduction to naval life.

HMS *Fisgard*
Royal Naval Apprentices Training Establishment, Torpoint, for newly-joined technical and engineering ratings.

HMS *Thunderer*
The Royal Naval Engineering College, Manadon is the Navy's technical university to the northeast of the Dockyard.

HMS *Cambridge*
The Royal Naval Gunnery Range at Wembury on the coast, some five miles to the east of Plymouth Sound.

Royal Naval Armament Depot, Bull Point
Almost under the Tamar Bridge.

Royal Naval Armament Depot, Ernesettle
North of the Dockyard.

Royal Naval Arament Depot, Stonehouse
Between Devonport and Plymouth.

Royal William Victualling Yard
This was built in 1826-35 by Sir John Rennie who was also responsible for the construction of the Breakwater in 1811-44. It is now HM Victualling Depot and is located near the Cremyll Ferry.

Plymouth is the Headquarters of the Royal Marine Commando Forces, the 3rd Commando Brigade being based here. It comprises: the Headquarters Signals Squadron; the Logistic Regiment; and 40, 41, 42 and 45 Commandos. Plymouth is ideally situated for training exercises on both the coast and on Dartmoor, sometimes described as England's last wilderness. The Royal Marines' traditional home in the area is Stonehouse Barracks, founded in 1784 and considerably enlarged in the middle of the 19th century.

Vantage Points
Close-up views of shipping movements can be obtained from any publicly accessible spot from Plymouth Hoe round to Mount Wise, Devil's Point and the Cremyll Ferry. There are a number of corresponding points on the Cornish shore of the Tamar on the Mount Edgecumbe Estate. There are 'trips round the harbour' from Sutton Pool (The Barbican), while vessels awaiting disposal can be seen from the Tamar Bridge and its approaches. The Type 61 frigate *Salisbury* is used as a harbour training ship by HMS *Raleigh*. More distant views of vessels entering and leaving Plymouth can be obtained from both sides of the Sound. *(The nearest railway stations in the area are Plymouth, Devonport, Keyham, St Budeaux — Ferry Road and Victoria Road stations — and Saltash.)*

Culdrose

HMS *Seahawk*, the Royal Naval Air Station at Culdrose outside Helston in Cornwall, was established during World War 2. It is now the home of the Royal Naval Helicopter School; the Royal Naval School of Aircraft Handling; the Royal Naval Flying Training School; the Royal Naval Aircrewman's School; and the Royal Naval School of Meteorology & Oceanography. As these titles indicate, rotary-winged aircraft are the predominant machines operated, and the following types can usually be seen flying over the Lizard Peninsula and the surrounding waters: Westland Gazelle (705 Squadron, pilot training); Westland Sea King Mk 5 (706 Squadron, aircrew training); and Westland Wessex Mk 5 (771 Squadron, search and rescue). There are also the British Aerospace Jetstream fixed-wing aircraft of 750 Squadron, used for observer training. *(Public Open Day in summer; Tel (032-65) 4121.)*

Yeovilton

The Royal Naval Air Station known as HMS *Heron* was established some five miles north of Yeovil in Somerset, during World War 2, serving as a fighter training airfield and fighter direction school. After the war its facilities expanded to meet the growing speeds and complexities of the jet age. It is now the home of Naval Air Squadrons 800, 801 and 899 (British Aerospace Sea Harrier FRS1); 707 (Westland Wessex Mk 5 for aircrew training with the Aircraft Direction School); 845 (Westland Wessex Mk 5 for Commando Assault); 846 (Westland Sea King Mk 4 for Commando Assault); and the Fleet Requirements and Aircraft Direction Unit (Hawker Hunters and English Electric Canberras). FRADU provides the guide aircraft for radio-controlled drones, act as targets for radar and armament calibration, and undertakes aerial photography during exercises. It also gives aircraft direction officers experience during their training. Seagoing Harrier and front line helicopter squadrons come to Yeovilton when not embarked on their carriers.

HMS *Heron* is also the flagship of the Flag Officer, Naval Air Command. This means that FONAC's headquarters flight of liaison aircraft is based here (de Havilland Herons). The Flag Officer's personal aircraft is known as 'The Admiral's Barge'.

In addition, Yeovilton is the base of 3 Commando Brigade Air Squadron, equipped with Westland Lynx and Gazelle helicopters for ground attack, and aerial observation and liaison duties.

Most types of Fleet Air Arm aircraft call at Yeovilton at some time, as well as temporary visitors from other air forces. They can all be seen from the free car park and public enclosure outside the Museum. *(Public Open Day in early August; Tel (0935) 840565.)*

Other establishments in England

Deal

The Royal Marines' Depot in Kent.

Herstmonceux Castle

This Sussex castle was built in 1300, fortified in 1440 and demolished in 1770. Herstmonceux Castle was reconstructed and restored in 1913-33 and in 1948 became the home of the Royal Observatory which was transferred from Greenwich. Its links with the Royal Navy's navigation are retained because the castle accommodates the Navy's Chronometer Section.

HMS *Dauntless*

The Women's Royal Naval Service Training Establishment at Burghfield near Reading in Berkshire.

Holton Heath

The Admiralty Materials Laboratory near Poole in Dorset.

Poole

Royal Marines' Amphibious Depot.

Lympstone
The Royal Marines' Commando Training Centre near Exeter in Devon.

Exeter
Royal Naval Stores Depot.

Taunton
The headquarters of the Navy's Hydrographic Department is located just outside the county town of Somerset.

HMS *Royal Arthur*
The Royal Naval Petty Officers' Training School at Corsham in Wiltshire.

Wroughton
The Royal Naval Aircraft Yard near Swindon in Wiltshire.

Bath
Ministry of Defence and Royal Navy offices were originally established in this city as part of the government's dispersal of Civil Service departments during World War 2.

Inskip
Royal Naval Wireless-Telegraphy Station near Preston in Lancashire.

Forest Moor
Royal Naval Wireless-Telegraphy Station at Darley near Harrogate in Yorkshire. These two establishments are typical representatives of the Navy's worldwide communications network.

Eaglescliffe
Spare Parts Distribution Centre, near Stockton-on-Tees in Cleveland.

Broughton Moor
Royal Naval Armament Depot near Maryport in Cumbria.

Dyfed (Wales)

Llangennech
Royal Naval Stores Depot, four miles east of Llanelli.

Pembroke Dock
HM Oil Fuel Depot. This is also one of the places away from the main ports where vessels awaiting disposal and scrapping may be seen.

Milford Haven
Royal Naval Armament Depot.

Trecwn
Royal Naval Armament Depot five miles south of Fishguard.

Above:
This view of an air display over Southsea Common shows all the vantage points for watching warships entering or leaving Portsmouth Harbour. Southsea Castle and the RN Portsmouth Division War Memorial can be seen in the foreground, then the trace and moat of De Gomme's 17th century fortifications, with Portsmouth Cathedral and HMS *Vernon* to the right. On the farther shore are the distinctive square shape of the Submarine Escape Training Tower, and the black silhouettes of submarines berthed alongside HMS *Dolphin* at Fort Blockhouse. Farther to the right, beyond the Gosport Ferry pontoon and marina, can be seen the Royal Clarance Victualling Yard and the beginnings of the Royal Navy Armament Depot, Gosport. The ships leaving harbour are a 'County' class destroyer, and three frigates — a 'Leander', a Type 21 'A' class, and another 'Leander'. This photograph was taken in 1979, before the opening of the D-Day Museum by Southsea Castle.

Below:
HMS *Sirius* (a 'Leander' class frigate) passing Mount Edgecumbe as she leaves Devonport in February 1984.

Above:
HMS *Orpheus* in the Clyde estuary in January 1978.

Left:
The French submarine *Dauphin* represents those foreign vessels which can be seen entering and leaving British ports, and are sometimes open to visitors during Navy Days and on other special occasions. This photograph was taken at Rosyth Dockyard on 19 May 1979. *A. Denholm*

Below:
'Ton' class MCMVs at Gibraltar in May 1984. Three of those nearest the harbour wall are (right to left): *Alfriston*, *Shavington* and *Kellington*. Note the twin-funnelled harbour berthing tug.

Faslane

HMS *Neptune* is the name of the Royal Navy's submarine base at Faslane on the Gare Loch, one of the narrow inlets at the northern head of the Firth of Clyde. The Commodore-in-Charge is also responsible for the defence of the Clyde and for liaison with merchant shipping movements. He has under his command the Royal Naval Officer Greenock and the 2nd Boom Defence Squadron. These vessels lay, maintain and patrol, huge steel nets which hang vertically below the surface to enmesh any unauthorised submersible attempting to enter the anchorage. Merchantmen can shelter behind such defences, for the Clyde would be a vital port in an emergency of any duration. However, these boom defences are principally for the protection of the nuclear-powered boats of the 3rd and 10th Submarine Squadrons which operate from Faslane and are the reason for the existence of the base.

The 10th Squadron is composed of 'R' class vessels capable of launching Polaris missiles; they are Britain's nuclear deterrent force. They will eventually be replaced by the projected Trident-firing SSBNs.

The 3rd Submarine Squadron has boats from the 'S', 'T', and 'Valiant' classes. These are designed to stalk and destroy hostile ships, especially enemy submarines carrying ballistic missiles aimed at targets in the NATO area.

'O' class boats also serve in the 3rd Submarine Squadron for patrol in waters too restricted for the deep-diving nuclear vessels.

The 10th Squadron submarines are provided with two complete crews each. One crew takes the boat to sea, remaining submerged for several months. Meanwhile the other crew is on leave or undergoing refresher courses, either at one of the appropriate schools or at the Submarine Sea Training Unit which is also based at Faslane. The majority of submarine movements likely to be seen off Faslane are most probably connected with these exercises. Just occasionally one of the operational boats may be glimpsed departing for or returning from her secret patrol area, but there is no way of telling the difference between that and a training exercise.

Vantage Points

Publicly accessible places on either side of the Gare Loch. *(Nearest railway station: Garelochhead.)*

Prestwick

The Royal Naval unit based at Prestwick Airport is known as HMS *Gannet*. It comprises 819 Squadron, operating Westland Sea King Mk 5 helicopters. These are used for anti-submarine patrols over the Firth of Clyde and the approaches to the nuclear submarine bases at Faslane (RN) and Holy Loch (USN).

Vantage Points

Spectator facilities are accessible via lift or stairs to a terrace on the second floor of the airport building. *Opening hours:* 07.00-20.00 summer/07.00-17.00 winter. *Admission charge:* 5p. Car park available. *Tel (0292)-79822 ext 4011/4051. Nearest station: Prestwick.*

In the Clyde Area

Beith
Royal Naval Armament Depot 10 miles southwest of Paisley.

Old Kilpatrick
HM Oil Fuel Depot on the Clyde between Glasgow and the sea.

Helensburgh
Admiralty Research Laboratory Extension in Glen Fruin.

Coulport
Royal Naval Armament Depot near HMS *Neptune*.

Loch Long
Royal Naval Torpedo Range at Arrochar.

Loch Goil
Admiralty Research Laboratory Extension.

Loch Striven
NATO POL Depot (for petrol, oil and lubricants).

Campbeltown
NATO POL Depot.

Rosyth

The Firth of Forth was the home of the Royal Scottish Navy under the Stewarts. After the Union with England, its significance as a naval base declined, ports farther south being better positioned for warfare against the French. However, the Firth of Forth retained its importance for trade with the Baltic and Scandinavia. Then, in 1914, the new weapons of mine and torpedo seemed to prohibit the close blockade of the enemy's coasts. Scapa Flow in the Orkneys was therefore selected as the Royal Navy's main operational base. From there the Grand Fleet could block any attempt by the German High Seas Fleet to break out into the Atlantic. However, events proved that Scapa Flow was too far north for easy interception of German warships with more limited objectives in the North Sea, such as raiding the East Coast of England. Accordingly an advanced base was established for the fast capital ships of Beatty's Battlecruiser Fleet, at Rosyth near the Forth Bridge, where a dockyard had been under construction since before the war. The escorting destroyers were berthed at Port Edgar, next to South Queensferry. Work on the dockyard was accelerated in 1918, and Rosyth became the main operational base for the whole of the Grand Fleet.

The official title of the Rosyth Naval Base today is HMS *Cochrane*. It is the headquarters of the Flag Officer, Scotland and Northern Ireland, whose NATO designation is 'COMNORECHAN & COMNOREASTLANT'. He is responsible for operations from the English Channel to Iceland and along the coast of Norway. This is in effect NATO's northern flank, being the area through which Soviet warships (surface and submerged) would have to pass to threaten transatlantic traffic. It is intended that a twin-deck complex will be built at Rosyth to refit the projected Trident submarines when they enter service. HMS *Cochrane* is also the flagship of the admiral, responsible for the local defence of the Firth of Forth. *(Public Navy Days in summer; Tel (0383)-2121.)*

Other naval establishments in the area are:

HMS *Caledonia*
Royal Marine Engineering School, which is part of the Rosyth complex.

Royal Naval Armament Depot, Crombie
Adjacent to Rosyth.

Royal Elizabeth Yard
HM Victualling Depot at Kirkliston, three miles inland to the south of the Forth.

Dunfermline
Royal Naval Construction Research Establishment.

Turnhouse
Joint Maritime Operational Training Staff at RAF Turnhouse between Kirkliston and Edinburgh.

Vantage Points
The old ferry hards at North and South Queensferry in the shadow of the two Forth Bridges. Warships proceeding on northern patrol may be seen, besides their associated RFAs and the 1st Mine Counter-Measures Squadron (which also serves as a Fishery Protection Squadron). Vessels here awaiting scrapping include the old landing ships *Lofoten* and *Stalker*, and HMS *Dreadnought* — the Royal Navy's first nuclear-powered submarine, but now a quarter of a century old and at the end of her useful life. Some of these ships will be scrapped at Inverkeithing, a commercial breaker's yard nearby, which handles many old vessels from all over the world. *(Nearest stations: Dalmeny, North Queensferry and Inverkeithing.)*

Other Establishments in Scotland

Glen Douglas
NATO Ammunition Depot at Inverbeg in what was formerly Lanarkshire.

Perth
Royal Naval Aircraft Workshops.

Invergordon
HM Oil Fuel Depot on the Cromarty Firth.

Loch Ewe

NATO POL Depot in Northwest Scotland.

HMS *Vulcan*

The Royal Naval Nuclear Propulsion Test and Training Establishment at Dounreay on the northernmost coast of Scotland.

Miscellaneous Places at Home and Abroad

The Royal Navy continually maintains liaison with other services, departments and industry, so naval representatives and offices may be seen anywhere in the country, although not necessarily in uniform or with the building wearing the White Ensign.

Similarly, Royal Naval warships may be seen at any accessible port, either on goodwill visits or proceeding to or from privately-owned shipyards where they have been built or refitted. Courtesy calls are also made on the ports of friendly nations, so even on foreign holiday it is possible to see the Royal Navy.

In addition, a number of overseas bases are still maintained, although their dockyard facilities have been closed down or transferred to local ownership.

Bermuda

HMS *Malabar* is the official title of the RN establishment on Ireland Island, one of the isles making up the Bermuda archipelago. Construction of the dockyard on Ireland Island began in 1810. It became the base of the Royal Navy's America & West Indies Squadron, being used for operations against pirates and slavers, and later serving in two world wars. It was closed as a royal dockyard in 1951, but the Navy still maintains a presence there. Bermuda would be a vital base for the protection of transatlantic shipping in an emergency. Its present significance to NATO lies in employment as a US air base (largely concerned with the defence of American waters against Soviet nuclear-powered missile-firing submarines). Bermuda is also the site of an American space vehicle tracking station. Although neither of these facilities is located on Ireland Island, the Royal Naval establishment liaises with them. And as Bermuda is a Crown Colony, the Navy is obviously closely involved in the defence of the group. So the Commanding Officer of HMS *Malabar* is also Deputy Island Commander.

Vantage Points

Bermuda serves as a centre for RN and other NATO warships on winter shakedown cruises after trials nearer their home bases. Such visitors often berth right alongside the Hamilton waterfront and can thus be seen at very close quarters.

Gibraltar

Gibraltar was captured by Sir George Rooke in 1704. Since then 'The Rock' has played an important part on every war fought by the British Navy.

Sometimes it has been a front-line operational base, and sometimes it has served as a staging-post for more distant campaigns.

At present the admiral at Gibraltar (officially termed HMS *Rooke*) is also NATO's COMGIBMED, responsible for operations in the Atlantic approaches to the Straits and in the western Mediterranean. Large stocks of fuel, stores and ammunition are held in surface installations and in underground caverns, for warships assigned to the Mediterranean, the Atlantic, or proceeding to the Falklands or the Indian Ocean and Far East. Gibraltar is also a suitable location for inter-service and inter-navy exercises, with Mediterranean and Atlantic forces taking it in turns to act as attacker and defender.

Vantage Points

Although Gibraltar does not now have a large fleet permanently based there, it is visited by many warships which either berth alongside or anchor in Gibraltar Bay. The dockyard itself is obviously a restricted place; middle-distance views of the ships can be obtained from any publicly accessible road on the western slopes of the rock.

Hong Kong

The Royal Navy has been protecting British interests in Chinese waters from this base since the middle of the 19th century. It is now represented by the 6th Patrol Squadron which inspects local vessels for smugglers and illegal immigrants. The RN base at Hong Kong is officially entitled HMS *Tamar*, other warships calling there besides the 'Peacock' class patrol vessels of the 6th Patrol Squadron.

Vantage Points

Anywhere along the Hong Kong waterfront, while more distant views can be obtained from Victoria Peak.

North America

RN officers and ratings serving as liaison personnel with the Canadian and American forces (the latter including Supreme Allied Commander Atlantic — SACLANT) are said to be assigned to HMS *Howard* (Ottawa) or HMS *Saker* (Washington).

The Ships and Aircraft of the Royal Navy

This section is divided into the following sub-sections:

- Submarines (usually painted black).
- Surface warships and Royal Fleet Auxiliaries —RFAs (both usually painted grey).
- Harbour and reserve craft (usually with black hulls while upperworks are buff-yellow or blue-grey respectively).
- Pennant numbers.
- Helicopters.
- Fixed-wing aircraft.

Within the first three sub-sections the classes are arranged in order of size according to standard (surfaced) tonnage displacement, measured in metric tons (t), although some vessels of mercantile appearance and function may be measured in British gross registered tons (grt). Dimensions for length, beam and draught are overall measurements in metres (m). Variations from these norms (eg, full load tonnage, deep draught, imperial measurements) are stated as such.

The name of each class is given, the dates quoted being when the first one was laid down and when the most recent was completed. Then follows a list of the ships in the class, plus their pennant numbers. These are not usually painted on submarines, although the name is sometimes displayed when entering or leaving harbour.

The appearance of the class is then described, starting from the bow. Then follows further information regarding other armament or equipment not obviously visible. Speed is usually the maximum, most vessels cruising at something like half that or even less; it is quoted in knots (kt), or nautical miles per hour. As one nautical mile (nm) equals approximately one minute of latitude measured along a meridian of longitude, it is thus possible to estimate fairly quickly a ship's passage across a chart or map. Endurance is not given, as most Royal Navy ships now customarily fuel at sea to extend their range without reliance on shore bases.

The number in the crew (complement) may vary according to circumstances. Present policy is to introduce as much labour-saving automation as possible, but this can result in having to accommodate the extra personnel needed to operate the additional items of miniaturised equipment which can thus be installed. And in an emergency, more crew may have to be embarked to cope with the additional work involved in extra signalling and the greater likelihood of having to implement damage control procedures.

Each class description includes notes on the function of that particular type.

All this information relates to ships in service or seaworthy reserve. Older vessels used as stationary harbour training ships or awaiting disposal for scrap, receive only the briefest mention.

The last two sub-sections are arranged in order of unladen weight in tonnes (t). Overall dimensions are span of rotor blades/wings×length in metres (m). A brief description of each type's appearance is given, plus an account of its role, armament, engines and crew. Speed is in knots (kt) and range in nautical miles (nm).

Note: This section is intended to help the reader identify ships and aircraft, and to explain something about whatever he or she is looking at. It is not intended as a definitive, comprehensive reference work. For such information, the reader is advised to turn to the Jane's series of yearbooks and to reference volumes published by Ian Allan Ltd.

Submarines

'R' class
1964-69

Resolution	(S22)	*Renown*	(S26)
Repulse	(S23)	*Revenge*	(S27)

Displacement: 7,620t
Dimensions: 129.5×10.1×9.1m
Arrangement: Long whale-shaped hull with higher profile than other submarines; bow planes hinge vertically on surface; conning-tower (fin or sail) has single thick standard with dome aft; note distinctive drop at end of hull casing covering 16 vertical tubes for launching Polaris ballistic missiles (each has a range of 2,500nm and carries three nuclear warheads which separate over hostile territory to take their own individual routes to their pre-arranged targets); the vertical rudder right aft seems to be separated from the boat.
Other armament: Six 21in (533mm) torpedo tubes capable of firing the Tigerfish electrically-propelled torpedo, with a reported range of 11nm. It is wire-guided from the submarine until close enough to the target for its own acoustic homing devices to take over.
Main engines: One pressurised water-cooled nuclear reactor producing steam for geared turbines driving one propeller shaft. Most nuclear submarines also have diesel and battery-driven electric motors for emergency propulsion on or below the surface respectively. Indeed, most warships have a variety of auxiliary machinery so that certain functions (eg ventilation, lighting, some armament, communications and damage control) can be maintained independently of the engine room. This is not only of vital importance in a battle, but is also useful when shore power facilities are not available and the main engines have been shut down.
Speed: 20kt (25kt submerged).
Complement: 143.
Notes: Officially designated SSBN (Nuclear-Powered Ballistic Missile

Submarine), the 'R' class is Britain's contribution to nuclear deterrence. Each boat is assigned a secret patrol area from whence missiles could be launched at targets allocated and ordered by the British government, in co-operation with its allies.

A new class of SSBNs should be entering service in the mid-1990s. Their Trident missiles will have a greater range than Polaris, each missile being fitted with 13 nuclear warheads.

'Valiant' class
1962-71

Valiant (S102)	Churchill (S46)	Courageous (S50)
Warspite (S103)	Conqueror (S48)	

Displacement: 4,870t
Dimensions: 86.9×10.1×8.2m
Arrangement: Whale-shaped hull with pronounced downwards curve aft; fin has two small standards and one tall (although these may not be apparent due to retraction or refit); rudder low down in wake.
Armament: Six 21in (533mm) torpedo tubes capable of firing Tigerfish torpedoes (in common with other fleet submarines, may also be fitted with Sub-Harpoon, an anti-ship missile with radar homing and a reported range of 50nm).
Main engines: One pressurised water-cooled nuclear reactor producing steam for geared turbines, driving one propeller shaft.
Speed: 28kt (submerged)
Complement: 103
Notes: These are designated as fleet submarines intended for the destruction of enemy warships, including submerged missile-carrying submarines. Fleet submarines can operate in any part of the global ocean, including beneath the Arctic ice. Like most modern submarines they are covered with anechoic (an/echo/ic) material. This may be in the form of solidified paste, or in the form of titles, or a combination of both. Its purpose is threefold: it smoothes the passage of the boat through the water; it reduces the sonar reflection of the hull; and it helps to seal noise in — each factor lessening the chance of underwater location by enemy detection devices.

'S' class
1969-81

Swiftsure (S126)	Superb (S109)	Spartan (S105)
Sovereign (S108	Sceptre (S104)	Spendid (S106)

Displacement: 4,270t
Dimensions: 82.9×9.8×8.2m
Arrangement: Whale-shaped hull, top of casing appearing to be level; fin has one short and one tall standard; rudder 'sits on top of' stern.
Armament: Five 21in (533mm) torpedo tubes for Tigerfish torpedoes.
Speed: 30+kt submerged
Complement: 97
Notes: Fleet submarines with same role and other details as 'Valiant' class.

'T' class
1978 —

Trafalgar (S107)	*Tireless* (S117)	*Trenchant* (S115)
Turbulent (S110)	*Torbay* (S118)	*Tactician* (S...)

Displacement: 4,000t
Dimensions: 85.4×9.8×8.2m
Speed: 32kt submerged
Notes: Fleet submarines with same role and other details as 'S' class.

Dreadnought
1959-63
Dreadnought (S101)

Displacement: 3,050t
Arrangement: Whale-shaped hull; bow planes at angle to hull.
Notes: The Royal Navy's first nuclear-powered vessel, but now obsolescent and at Rosyth awaiting disposal.

'O' class
1957-67

Oberon (S09)	*Onslaught* (S14)	*Opossum* (S19)
Odin (S10)	*Otter* (S15)	*Opportune* (S20)
Orpheus (S11)	*Oracle* (S16)	*Onyx* (S21)
Olympus (S12)	*Ocelot* (S17)	
Osiris (S13)	*Otus* (S18)	

Displacement: 1,640t
Dimensions: 90×8.1×5.5m
Arrangement: Much more angular than nuclear submarines; sonar dome forward; bow planes hinge vertically; Series 800 surveillance radar carried but not apparent; fin may display items of equipment carried for testing or instruction before fitting in nuclear submarines.
Armament: Six 21in (533mm) torpedo tubes forward. (These fire the Mk 8 torpedo, a well-proven and reliable design introduced in the 1930s. Driven by an internal combustion engine breathing compressed air, the Mk 8 has a range of 2.5nm at 45kt. It can also be issued to nuclear submarines instead of the Tigerfish torpedo. Two 21in tubes aft fire the shorter Mk 20 electrically-driven sonar-homing torpedo. For use against submerged targets, it has a range of 5.5nm at 20kt.
Main engines: Two diesels and two electric motors, each set driving one propeller shaft.
Speed: 12kt (17kt submerged)
Complement: 69
Notes: Designated Patrol submarines, the 'O' class is intended for service in waters too restricted in every dimension for nuclear boats.

'Porpoise' class

1954-61

Sealion (S07)
Walrus (S08)

Notes: Virtually identical to 'O' class, except for a complement of 71.

Finwhale (S05) is now awaiting disposal and scrapping. *Porpoise* (S01) has been painted bright red as an expendable target for the Spearfish torpedo trials at Faslane.

Type 2400

New Patrol Submarine
Displacement: 2,400t submerged
Dimensions: 50×7.6×5.5m
Armament: In shape like a small nuclear-powered submarine. Six 21in (533mm) torpedo tubes forward.
Main engines: Two diesels and one electric motor, together driving one propeller shaft.
Speed: 20kt submerged
Complement: 46
Notes: The first of these projected submarines has now been ordered for possible completion in 1987. It is expected that they will perpetuate such famous World War 2 names as *Upholder*, *Ursula*, *Untiring*, etc.

Warships and RFAs

Projected RFAs

Displacement: 30,000t
Armament: One 20mm gun; Sea Wolf anti-aircraft and anti-missile missile launchers.
Notes: It is intended that these new RFAs will be able to supply warships at sea with dry stores, fuel and ammunition, thus combining in one hull functions which have previously had to be carried out by three separate types of RFA.

Hermes

Aircraft Carrier (1944-59)
Hermes (R12)
Displacement: 24,280t
Dimensions: 226.9×27.4 (48.8 across flight deck) ×8.7m
Arrangement: Inclined ramp at bow for 'jump-jet' take-off; unobstructed flight-deck with sponsons and recesses; island on starboard side (bridge and solid mast carrying bedstead aerial for Type 984 three-dimensional long-range air-surveillance radar; funnel venting four oil-fuelled boilers providing steam for geared turbines driving two propeller shafts; lattice mast carrying wide, thin solid aerial for Type 992 general purpose radar; dish aerial at after end of island for GWS22 Seacat direction radar — the Seacat system has facilities for visual guidance in every ship in which it is

Right:
The nuclear-powered Polaris submarine HMS *Repulse* off Faslane.

Below:
The launch of the fleet submarine HMS *Turbulent*.

Bottom:
HMS *Dolphin*, the submarine base at Gosport, seen from the Royal Navy Submarine Museum on 8 August 1984. The pairs of submarines from left to right are: *Walrus* and *Otter*; and *Sealion* and *Osiris*. The nearer of the third pair (neither of their names being visible) has had part of its casing removed to enable work to be carried out on its engines. The stern of the midget submarine *X24* can be seen in the bottom right-hand corner. *Author*

Top:
**The aircraft carrier HMS *Illustrious*
with Wessex and Sea King helicopters
on her flightdeck.**

Above:
**A Westland Wessex helicopter over
HMS *Fearless*.** *Author's collection*

Left:
**A close-up of the A-frame on the stern
of the seabed operations vessel HMS
Challenger. This equipment is used for
deploying manned and unmanned
submersible craft.**

installed; two quadruple Seacat anti-aircraft missile launchers on sponsons right aft below flight-deck level. (The official title of the Seacat is Guided Weapons System Mk 20. It has a range of 2.5nm.)

Aircraft carried: Nine Hawker Siddeley Sea Harrier strike fighters; nine Westland Sea King Mk 5 anti-submarine helicopters; Westland Wessex Mk 5 Commando assault helicopters.

Speed: 28kt

Complement: 1,350 plus 750 Royal Marine Commandos plus another 750 RM Commandos in an emergency.

Notes: Served as an ocean-going base for airborne anti-submarine forces; *Hermes* also operated as an amphibious warfare ship, her Harriers providing strike cover for helicopter-borne commandos. The future of *Hermes* is in some doubt following her decommissioning.

'Invincible' class

Aircraft Carriers (1973-84)

Invincible   (R05)   *Ark Royal*   (R07)
Illustrious   (R06)

Displacement: 16,260t

Dimensions: 206.6×27.5 (31.9 across flight deck) ×7.3m

Arrangement: Bow lower than flight deck; one twin Sea Dart missile launcher (officially designated GWS Mk 30, the Sea Dart has a range of 15nm. Primarily an anti-aircraft weapon, it can also be used against surface vessels); flight deck starts here with an inclined ramp for 'jump-jet' take-off; rest of flight deck is unobstructed. Island on starboard side — radome containing Type 909 radar for Sea Dart guidance; bridge and solid mast carrying bedstead aerial for Type 1022 long-range search radar; solid mast; funnel venting two Bristol Olympus gas turbines; solid mast carrying wide, thin solid aerial for type 992 general purpose radar; funnel venting two Rolls-Royce Tyne cruising gas turbines. (Each set of one main and one cruising gas turbine, drives one shaft. Gas turbines were first introduced into warships larger than fast attack craft, to provide a means of getting under way without waiting to raise steam in oil-fuelled boilers. Gas turbines soon proved reliable enough to serve as main engines, smaller types such as the Tyne, being employed for more economical cruising. Gas turbines have the additional advantage in that they burn virtually the same fuel as that used in jet aircraft, which eases storage and fuelling at sea problems.) Two radomes containing satellite communication aerials; radome containing Type 909 radar for Sea Dart guidance.

These ships also carry Vulcan/Phalanx guns (two mounted forward and aft on the starboard side of the flight-deck in *Invincible* and *Illustrious*); each unit in this Close-In Weapons System (CIWS) has six barrels, for radar-directed barrage at the rate of 3,000 rounds per minute in the path of attacking aircraft and missiles. There are also two single 20mm Oerlikon GAM-B01 guns for manual fire against air and small surface targets.

Aircraft carried: Nine Westland Sea King Mk 5 anti-submarine helicopters; five Sea Harrier strike fighters.

Squadrons	Sea Harriers	Sea Kings
Invincible	801	820
Illustrious	809	814
Ark Royal		

Speed: 28kt
Complement: 900
Notes: Each of the 'Invincibles' serves as the centre of an anti-submarine task force. The armament, aircraft and radar fit of all three (indeed of all warships) can vary as they undergo refit.

'Fort' class

Fleet Replenishment Ships   (1973-79)
Fort Austin   (A386)
Fort Grange   (A385)

Displacement: 14,700t
Dimensions: 183.8×24×7.6m
Arrangement: Raised forecastle; single mast; well-deck with deckhouse and goalpost mast (plus booms); high, piled-up superstructure with bridge and solid mast; goalpost mast with derricks; funnel venting diesel driving one propeller shaft; cranes; goalpost mast with derricks; hangar and flightdeck for Westland Sea King helicopters.
Speed: 20kt
Complement: 185
Notes: RFAs intended to work with the Fleet, for under way transfer of 8,300t of stores and ammunition.

'Fearless' class
Assault Ships   (1962-67)
Fearless   (L10)
Intrepid   (L11)

Displacement: 11,240t
Dimensions: 158.5×24.4×6.2m (9.8m when flooded down to enable the landing craft to enter or leave the dock aft).
Arrangement: Raised deck carrying one quadruple Seacat missile launcher; bridge with one 40mm gun on each side; short, solid mast carrying (like the rest of the superstructure) communications equipment to enable the ship to act as the headquarters of an air/sea/land assault force; tall solid mast carrying quarter-cheese aerial for Type 993 air/sea search radar; tall funnel to port, venting boiler producing steam for geared turbine driving one propeller shaft; one quadruple Seacat missile launcher on each side of superstructure (plus control equipment and director); boats at davits include two LCVP on each side; one quadruple Seacat missile launcher at end of superstructure; short funnel to starboard venting boiler for producing steam

for geared turbine driving one propeller shaft; flight deck for five Westland Wessex helicopters; crane on port side of stern; stern door giving access to dock which contains four LCM(9).
Speed: 21kt
Complement: 550 plus troops
Notes: *Fearless* and *Intrepid* are virtually self-propelled ocean-going floating docks, able to put ashore 400-700 troops, 15 tanks, seven 3ton and 20 ¼ton vehicles, or any combination of these. They can also serve as sea-going training ships for Britannia Royal Naval College, Dartmouth.

'Ol' class
Large Fleet Tankers (1963-66)
Olmeda (A124)
Olna (A123)
Olwen (A122)

Displacement: 11,070t
Dimensions: 197.5×25.6×10.3m
Arrangement: Single mast and derrick (or goalpost mast); bridge with mast; well-deck with pumping equipment and four goalpost masts carrying refuelling booms; after superstructure; funnel venting boilers producing steam for geared turbines driving one propeller shaft; hangar and flight deck for four Westland Sea King helicopters.
Speed: 19kt
Complement: 87
Notes: For rapid oiling of ships at sea, without their having to reduce from cruising speed. Some stores are also carried and can be transferred in similar fashion. Total weight of cargo is over 22,000t. Manned as RFAs.

'Re' class
Fleet Replenishment Ships (1964-67)
Regent (A486)
Resource (A480)

Displacement: 19,310t full load
Dimensions: 195.1×23.5×7.9m
Arrangement: Raised forecastle drops one level; mast and derrick; goalpost mast; bridge with mast; four sets of goalpost masts and derricks; raised poop; after superstructure; funnel venting boilers producing steam for geared turbines driving one propeller shaft; hangar and flight deck for Westland Sea King helicopters.
Speed: 20kt
Complement: 182
Notes: These two ships are manned by a combination of RFA crew, stores-issuing Civil Servants, and FAA personnel. Food, explosives, ammunition and stores can all be transferred at sea.

Tiger
Cruiser (1941-59)
Tiger (C20)

Displacement: 9,650t
Arrangement: Two gun turrets forward; bridge, mast and funnel; space; funnel; mast and box-like hangar; flight-deck at stern.
Notes: Converted as a helicopter-cruiser in 1968-72, *Tiger* is now at Portsmouth awaiting disposal for scrap.

'Head' class
Maintenance Ships (1944-45)
Rame Head (A134)
Berry Head (A191)

Displacement: 9,100t
Arrangement: Mercantile hull with raised plating at forecastle and amidships; deckhouses along most of hull; crane forward; lattice mast abaft bridge; single funnel; derricks aft.
Notes: *Rame Head* is alongside at Rosyth; *Berry Head* is an accommodation ship at Devonport.

'Tide' class
Large fleet tankers (1961-63)
Tidespring (A75)

Displacement: 8,670t
Dimensions: 177.7×21.6×9.7m
Arrangement: Goalpost mast plus derricks; bridge with mast; well-deck with pumping equipment and three goalpost masts plus oiling booms; poop deck with superstructure; funnel venting boilers for geared turbines driving one propeller shaft; hangars and flight deck for helicopters.
Speed: 17kt
Complement: 110
Notes: This RFA can transfer some 13,000t of fuel and 4,000t of stores.

Engadine
Helicopter Support Ship (1965-67)
Engadine (K08)

Displacement: 8,130t
Dimensions: 129.3×17.7×6.7m
Arrangement: Mercantile mast on forecastle; passenger-liner appearance of superstructure, with bridge merging into hangar; hull drops one level from forecastle, but is screened by bulwarks; solid mast abaft bridge; one funnel venting diesel engine driving one shaft; unobstructed flight deck aft, for four Westland Wessex and two Wasp *or* two Sea King helicopters.
Speed: 14.5kt
Complement: 63 RFA personnel plus 14 permanent RN plus 113 trainees

Notes: *Engadine* is operated by the RFA service; her crew is civilian and her name is on her bow. She is intended as an ocean-going training ship for helicopter personnel, thus obviating the need for a warship to be taken off active operations to perform such a duty. She can also launch pilotless aircraft as exercise targets.

Engadine will be paid off when a replacement helicopter support ship enters service. Laid down as the mercantile *Contender Bezant*, the new vessel will be named *Argus* after conversion.

Challenger
Seabed Operations Vessel (1979-83)
Challenger (K07)

Displacement: 7,315t
Dimensions: 134.1×18×5.5m
Arrangement: Hull merges into superstructure and square bridge well forward with goalpost mast; drops near cranes; twin funnels aft (venting five diesels, powering electric motors which drive two vertical Voith-Schneider propellers aft and three bow thrusters forward).
Speed: 15kt
Complement: 185
Notes: Can launch submersibles and other deep-ocean equipment, either from an A-frame and ramp at the stern, or via a moonpool amidships.

New 'Leaf' class
Support Tankers (1974-79)
Appleleaf (A79)
Bayleaf (A109)
Brambleleaf (A81)

Displacement: 6,910t
Dimensions: 170.7×25.9×11.9m
Arrangement: Flush-deck with flying-deck covering pumping equipment; short mast forward; small bridge and goalpost mast amidships, plus oiling booms; derricks; raised poop with piled-up superstructure, mast and funnel (venting two diesels, together driving one propeller shaft).
Speed: 15.5-16.3kt
Notes: Although RFA support tankers can oil ships at sea, their main functions are the regular delivery of 33,000t of cargo to fleet replenishment tankers and the provision of refuelling facilities in remote harbours with inadequate shore installations. Oiling can be conducted simultaneously on both sides and over the stern.

The merchant tanker *Balder London* is being converted for service as RFA *Orangeleaf*.

Old 'Leaf' class
Support Tankers (1959-60)
Plumleaf (A78)
Pearleaf (A77)

Displacement: 6,460-6,970t
Dimensions: 170.7-173.1×21.9×9.1m
Arrangement: Raised forecastle; forward well-deck with catwalk over pumping equipment; pole mast and derrick (*Plumleaf*) or goalpost mast (*Pearleaf*); hull plating rises amidships under bridge; pole mast; goalpost mast with refuelling booms; after well-deck with catwalk over pumping equipment; derrick; poop deck with after superstructure; funnel venting diesel driving one propeller shaft.
Speed: 15½kt
Complement: 55
Notes: RFAs capable of delivering more than 18,000t of oil, aviation fuel and other POL to warships and fleet replenishment tankers in remote locations.

Bristol
Type 82 Light Cruiser/Destroyer (1967-73)
Bristol   (D23)

Displacement: 6,100t
Dimensions: 154.5×16.8×6.9m
Arrangement: One 4.5in (114mm) Mk 8 gun with a range of 6.5nm in a round fully-automatic turret; deckhouse; one Ikara launcher, often under a hemispherical cover (the Ikara missile has a range of 13nm; it releases a Mk 46 aerial torpedo which homes on to an enemy submarine); radome covering Type 909 radar for Sea Dart guidance; bridge with a small dome on each side covering aerials for satellite communication; one 20mm gun on each side; solid mast with bedstead aerial for Type 965 long-range search radar; funnel venting oil-fired boilers producing steam for two sets of geared turbines; solid mast with thin, narrow aerial for Type 992 general purpose radar; two funnels side by side, each venting one Olympus gas turbine (each set of one steam and one gas turbine drives one propeller shaft); radome covering Type 909 radar; deck drops one level here; one twin Sea Dart launcher.
Speed: 28kt
Complement: 407
Notes: *Bristol* can also operate a Westland Wasp helicopter, but it is not usually carried. She was intended as the first of a class of aircraft carrier escorts, but the abandonment of that particular carrier programme also entailed the cancellation of further Type 82s.

'County' class
Light Cruisers/Destroyers (1960-70)
Glamorgan   (D19)
Fife   (D20)

Displacement: 5,530t
Dimensions: 158.7×16.5×6.3m
Arrangement: One twin 4.5in (114mm) mounting in a remotely-controlled square turret; one quadruple Exocet launcher for anti-ship missiles fitted with their own homing radar for the last stages of their 35nm, low-level flight; hull-plating here merges with the next deck up; bridge with dish

aerial for MRS3/GWS22 radar controlling 4.5in guns, intitial Exocet launch, and Seacat direction; single 20mm gun on each side of bridge; solid mast with thin, narrow aerial for Type 992 general purpose radar; funnel venting oil-fired boilers producing steam for two sets of geared steam turbines; solid mast carrying bedstead aerial for Type 965 long-range search radar, plus (below) dish aerial for Type 278 height-finder radar; funnel venting four gas turbines (each set of one geared turbine and two gas turbines drives one propeller shaft); hangar for one Westland Lynx Mk 2 anti-submarine helicopter; one quadruple Seacat launcher on each side of hangar; cylindrical aerial for Type 901 Seaslug guidance; deck drops two levels here; one twin launcher for Seaslug missiles which ride a beam emitted by the Type 901 radar to a distance of over 20nm and a height of 15,000m (it can also be used against ship targets).

Speed: 30kt
Complement: 472
Notes: The 'Counties' were designed to provide anti-aircraft protection for task forces. They would be disposed around the vital carriers or transports, and were thus also in a position to ward off attacks by surface vessels; hence the guns and Exocet which could also prove useful on detached service. The 'Counties' have been updated during their careers, but they are now obsolescent. Some have already been scrapped, transferred to other navies, or are awaiting disposal. *Kent* (D12) has been refitted as a Sea Cadet Corps accommodation ship at Portsmouth.

'Town' class
Type 42 Destroyers (1972-84)

Batch I
Birmingham (D86)
Newcastle (D87)
Glasgow (D88)
Cardiff (D108)

Batch II
Exeter (D89)
Southampton (D90)
Nottingham (D91)
Liverpool (D92)

Displacement: 3,560t
Dimensions: 125×14.3×5.8m

Batch III
Manchester (D95)
Gloucester (D96)
Edinburgh (D97)
York (D98)

Displacement: 4,780t
Dimensions: 141.1×14.9×5.8m
(longer forecastle)

Arrangement: One 4.5in (114mm) Mk 8 gun in round turret; one twin Sea Dart launcher; bridge with radome covering Type 909 radar for Sea Dart guidance; short, solid mast with bedstead aerial for Type 965 long-range search radar; solid mast with thin, narrow aerial on foretop for Type 1006 navigation radar; one single 20mm gun on each side of bridge; funnel venting two Olympus and two Tyne gas turbines (each set consisting of one of each type drives one propulsion shaft); one twin 30mm GCM-A01 gun mounting on each side of mast for use against aircraft and fast attack craft, with a range of 1.5nm; one triple set of 12.75in (324mm) torpedo tubes on each side for Mk 46 anti-submarine homing torpedoes with a range of 6nm; solid mast carrying thin, narrow aerial for Type 992 general purpose radar;

radome for Type 909 radar; hangar and flight deck for Westland Lynx Mk 2 helicopter; hull cut away under flight deck.
Speed: 29-30kt
Complement: 300-312
Notes: All three batches of the Type 42 'Towns' are intended to provide defence against aircraft, fast attack craft and other surface ships and submarines on the periphery of a group of ships: this may not necessarily be a task force with a particular assignment such as hunting a raider or preparing to assault a hostile shore. The 'Towns' — and indeed all other types of destroyers, frigates and escorts — could be similarly employed screening merchant ships.

'Rover' class
Small Fleet Tankers (1968-74)

| *Black Rover* | (A273) | *Gold Rover* | (A271) | *Grey Rover* | (A269) |
| *Blue Rover* | (A270) | *Green Rover* | (A268) | | |

Displacement: 4,530t
Dimensions: 140.5×19.2×7.3m
Arrangement: Raised forecastle; deckhouse with docking bridge and transfer control points; high goalpost mast with one refuelling boom on each side; well-deck with pumping equipment; pair of derricks; raised poop deck under lofty, piled-up superstructure with bridge, solid mast and tall funnel (venting two diesels, together driving one propeller shaft); goalpost mast with derricks; docking bridge with transfer control points; helicopter flight-deck.
Speed: 19kt
Complement: 47
Notes: Similar in function to the '01' class, but smaller. Capable of refuelling ships under way at sea in all weathers. At the same time a certain amount of fresh water (for drinking and for boiler feed water) and dry stores can be transferred — more than 7,000t total cargo. Helicopters can be used for vertical replenishment, and not only for ships in immediate company. *Blue Rover* is officially classified as a fleet replenishment ship, but there is virtually no difference in her appearance from the other RFAs in the class.

'B' class
Type 22 Frigates (1975-)
Batch I

| *Broadsword* | (F88) | *Brilliant* | (F90) |
| *Battleaxe* | (F89) | *Brazen* | (F91) |

Displacement: 3,560t
Dimensions: 131.2×14.8×4.3m

Batch II		*Sheffield*	(F96)
Boxer	(F92)	*Coventry*	(F..)
Beaver	(F93)		
Brave	(F94)	Batch III	
London	(F95)	*Cornwall*	(F..)

**The Type 82 destroyer HMS *Bristol*
firing a Sea Dart missile. Like the
'County' class ships, this vessel is
sometimes classed as a light cruiser.**

**HMS *Gloucester* at Portsmouth on
6 December 1984.** *Mike Lennon*

Bottom:
HMS *Nottingham*.

Below:
The Type 42 'Town' class destroyer

Above:
The small fleet tanker RFA *Blue Rover* with the Type 21 frigate HMS *Alacrity* to port and the 'Leander' class frigate HMS *Naiad* to starboard.

Left:
The Type 22 frigate HMS *Broadsword* entering Portsmouth Harbour in April 1979.

Below:
HMS *Boxer* is the first of the 'stretched' Type 22 frigates.

Chatham   (F..)
Cumbria   (F..) (or *Cumberland*)

Displacement: 4,170-4,270t
Dimensions: 143×14.8×4.3m

Arrangement: Batches II and III are known as Stretched Type 22s, being longer in the bow and bridge sections, and with a shorter funnel. Forecastle curves down under quadruple Exocet launcher (and one 4.5in Mk 8 round-turreted gun in Batch III only); deck rises here; one six-barrelled launcher for Sea Wolf anti-aircraft and anti-missile (and even anti-shell) missiles (GWS25) with a range of 3nm; bridge; radar array comprising two dish and one cylindrical aerial for Type 910 radar for Sea Wolf control; solid mast carrying thin, rectangular, solid aerial for radar Types 967 and 968 for air and sea surveillance; one 40mm gun with a range of 2nm (or one twin 30mm gun mounting in Batch III) on each side of mast; funnel venting two Olympus 9 (Spey in Batch III) and two Tyne gas turbines, each combined set driving one propeller shaft; one single 20mm gun on each side of superstructure; one triple set torpedo tubes for Mk 46 anti-submarine torpedoes on each side; solid mast; Type 910 radar array; one six-barrelled Sea Wolf launcher; hangar and flight deck for two Westland Lynx Mk 2 helicopters (EH101 in Batch III — which also have an additional Exocet launcher); hull cut away beside hangar (starboard side) and under flight deck for streaming variable depth sonar.
Speed: 30kt
Complement: 250-290
Notes: The 'B' class vessels are designed as general purpose frigates, suitable for independent action or for work with a task force. They can be used in either the anti-submarine, anti-aircraft or anti-ship role, although the last function is emphasised in the enhanced gunnery and Exocet armament of Batch III. The 'B' class would thus be very useful for defending merchant ships against raiders from above, on or below the sea.

Britannia
Royal Yacht (1952-54)
Britannia   (A00 — pennant number never displayed)

Displacement: 4,050t
Dimensions: 125.7×16.8×5.2m
Arrangement: Yacht-like appearance with royal blue hull and white superstructure; bridge; pole mast; buff funnel venting boilers producing steam for geared turbines driving two propeller shafts; pole mast; pole mast.
Speed: 21kt
Complement: 270 (commanded by Rear-Admiral Royal Yachts, not by a captain).
Notes: Designed for easy conversion to a wartime hospital ship, although this has never been done. Quite apart from providing accommodation for the Royal Family on state visits abroad, *Britannia* also serves as an administrative headquarters and logistics base on such occasions. And when proceeding to or from these locations, she acts as a single-ship convoy, providing escort experience for warships in company.

Type 23 Frigates

This project is still in the design stage; 12 may eventually be ordered. The first may be named *Norfolk*, the others having similar 'ducal' titles.

Displacement: 4,000t
Dimensions: 123×16.2×4.3m
Projected armament: 4.5in gun; 32 Sea Wolf anti-aircraft and anti-missile launchers; eight anti-ship launchers (Harpoon?); two other guns; anti-submarine torpedo tubes; two Westland EH101 helicopters.
Possible appearance: 4.5in gun mounting; SSM launchers; Sea Wolf launchers; bridge; Sea Wolf radar; mast; funnel (venting diesel-electric engines and gas turbines); mast; hangar and flight deck; variable depth sonar towed astern.
Speed: 28kt
Complement: 143-200
Notes: A general purpose frigate, some reports suggest she may have armour around certain vital areas, the first ship of the nuclear and missile age to be so fitted.

Endurance

Ice Patrol Ship (1955-56)
Endurance   (A171)

Displacement; 3,660t
Dimensions: 93×14×5.5m
Arrangement: Bright red flush deck, but curving hull (so painted to be easily visible in the Antarctic ice); derricks and bipod mast with crows nest (containing equipment to enable the ship to be conned through the ice from there); catwalk to bridge; one 20mm gun on each side; funnel venting diesel driving one propeller shaft; hangar and flight deck for two Westland Wasp helicopters.
Speed: 14.5kt
Complement: 119-131
Notes: *Endurance* is the Royal Navy's representative in the Antarctic, maintaining contact with British scientists, carrying out survey work, investigating natural phenomena and political incidents of all kinds, and generally 'showing the flag'.

'Sir Lancelot' class

Logistics Landing Ships (1962-68)

Sir Bedivere   (L3004)   *Sir Lancelot*   (L3029)   *Sir Tristram*   (L3505)
Sir Geraint   (L3027)   *Sir Percivale*   (L3036)

Displacement: 3,320t
Dimensions: 125.1×18.1×4m
Arrangement: Bow doors; high forecastle with (sometimes) one 40mm gun on each side; two derrick-type cranes; well-deck for 16 tanks, 34 other vehicles, 120t of POL, 30t ammunition; crane; hull rises aft; bridge and superstructure providing accommodation for 340-544 troops; mast; funnel venting two diesels, each driving one propeller shaft; helicopter flight deck; stern door and ramp.

Speed: 17kt
Complement: 68
Notes: These are RO/RO (roll-on/roll-off) ships, in which vehicles can be driven on at one end and be driven off at the other. These vessels can be beached, but do not normally do so, carrying powered pontoons to form a floating bridge from the ship to shore. They are RFAs with civilian crews. *Sir Tristram* is undergoing repair after considerable damage in the Falklands war.

A new *Sir Galahad* is on order (3,055t displacement; 140.5×19.5×4.3m).

Sir Lamorack
Logistics Landing Ship
Sir Lamorack (L3532)

Displacement: 2,540t deadweight
Dimensions: 108m length
Arrangement: Box-like hull with raking bow and square bridge right forward; one funnel on extreme edge of each side; stern door very prominent when stowed.
Notes: A Canadian RO/RO ship manned by a civilian crew and chartered by the Royal Navy until 1985.

Sir Caradoc (L3522) is another RO/RO ship similarly chartered until 1985, but of Norwegian nationality and of 3,560t deadweight. Such vessels are typical of those merchant Ships which have been Taken Up From Trade (STUFTs) during and since the Falklands war, for operations in that area. Some are commissioned with RN crews, while others (eg *Reliant* — A131) serve as RFAs, and others are chartered with their own crews. Some continue to function as merchantmen but on MoD business, and others serve as accommodation or repair ships (eg *Diligence*, ex-*Stena Inspector*). A few — particularly of trawler appearance — (eg *Protector*-P244, *Guardian*-P245, and *Sentinel*-P246) — have been adapted as minesweepers or patrol vessels. There is also HMS *Tiger Bay*, an ex-Argentinian coastal patrol craft of 80t, which was damaged and captured during the conflict. For a while she wore the White Ensign, but is now awaiting disposal.

'Leander' class
Frigates (1959-73)
Group I (Ikara)

Aurora (F10)	*Arethusa* (F38)	*Ajax* (F114)
Euryalus (F15)	*Naiad* (F39)	
Galatea (F18)	*Leander* (F109)	

Group II (Exocet/Towed Array)

Cleopatra (F28)	*Phoebe* (F42)
Sirius (F40)	*Argonaut* (F56)

Group II (Exocet)

Minerva (F45)	*Juno* (F52)
Danae (F47)	*Penelope* (F127)

Group III (Broad-Beamed Sea Wolf Conversion)
Andromeda (F57)   *Jupiter* (F60)   *Charybdis* (F75)
Hermione (F58)   *Scylla* (F71)

Group III (Broad-Beamed)
Achilles (F12)   *Apollo* (F70)
Diomede (F16)   *Ariadne* (F72)

Displacement: 2,450-2,540t
Dimensions: 113.4×12.5/13.1×5.5m
Arrangement: Forecastle slopes downwards;
Group I: Beginning of superstructure with Ikara launcher for anti-submarine missiles with homing torpedoes;
or
Groups II(TA) and II and III(BBC): One quadruple Exocet missile launcher;
or
Group III(BB): One twin 4.5in (115mm) gun mounting Mk 6 in square turret.
  Bridge with either one single 40mm or one twin 20mm plus one single 20mm on each side; MRS3/GWS22 radar array for gunnery and Exocet control (cocooned in Ikara ships); solid mast with quarter-cheese aerial for Type 993 surface and air warning radar; single 20mm GAM-BO1 gun here in Group III(BB) ships; funnel venting oil-fired boilers producing steam for two sets geared turbines, each set driving one propeller shaft; solid mast with bedstead aerial for Type 965 long-range search radar (removed from Group I); one quadruple Seacat anti-aircraft missile launcher on each side of mast (not in Groups III(BBC) and III(BB)); one set triple torpedo tubes for anti-submarine torpedoes on each side of superstructure (in Groups II (TA), II and III(BBC) only); GWS22 radar and optical director for Seacat; one quadruple Seacat launcher (in Group II and III(BB)), or one six-barrelled Sea Wolf launcher in Group III(BBC) — these last also have Type 910 radar; hangar and flight-deck for one Westland Lynx Mk 2 or Wasp helicopter; one triple-barrelled Limbo mortar for discharging anti-submarine depth-bombs to a radius of 0.5nm around the ship (in Group I and III(BB) only); equipment for towing variable depth sonar astern (in Group II(TA) only).
  There can be further differences in appearance and armament within the sub-groups, while some may be completely altered for some particular task. For example, *Juno* is being refitted as a Navigational Training and Direction Trials ship; when complete, she will be based at Portsmouth.
Speed: 28kt
Complement: 222-261
Notes: The 'Leanders' were general-purpose frigates originally, but the nature of the Ikara conversion has clearly made the Batch 1 ships suitable for the ASW role only.

'Rothesay' class
Modified Type 12 Frigates (1956-61)
Yarmouth (F101)   *Londonderry* (F108)   *Plymouth* (F126)
Lowestoft (F103)   *Falmouth* (F113)   *Rhyl* (F129)
Rothesay (F107)   *Berwick* (F115)

Displacement: 2,420t
Dimensions: 112.8×12.5×5.3m

Top:
A model of the possible appearance of the Type 23 frigate now being designed for the Royal Navy.

Above:
The ice patrol ship HMS *Endurance* and her Westland Wasp helicopter in the Antarctic pack.

Right:
RFA *Reliant* represents the STUFTs — Ships Taken Up From Trade. Note the Wessex helicopter on her deck.

Three 'Leander' class frigates:
Above:
HMS *Sirius*. *Mike Lennon*

Below:
HMS *Hermione* off Gosport in May 1983. *Mike Lennon*

Bottom:
HMS *Leander* firing an Ikara missile. *Mike Lennon*

Arrangement: Forecastle curves downwards under twin 4.5in (115mm) turret of square appearance; deck rises one level here and merges with bridge; two single 20mm guns on each side of superstructure; dish radar aerial array and director for MRS3 for gunnery control; solid mast carrying either quarter-cheese or nodding aerial for either Type 993 or Type 293 search radar; hull drops one level here; funnel venting oil-fired boilers producing steam for two sets geared turbines, each set driving one propeller shaft; Seacat control director; one quadruple Seacat missile launcher; hangar and flight deck for one Westland Wasp helicopter; one triple-barrelled Limbo mortar for launching anti-submarine depth-bombs (almost hidden in well); hull drops one level here.

Speed: 30kt
Complement: 235
Notes: Designed as anti-submarine escorts, the 'Rothesay' class now usually serves as general purpose patrol frigates. *Londonderry* is a stationary training ship at Portsmouth. *Falmouth* is a harbour training ship at Gosport. *Brighton* (F106) is at Rosyth awaiting scrapping.

The earlier Type 12 'Whitby' class is very similar. *Eastbourne* (F37) is a harbour training ship for engine-room personnel at Rosyth and will soon be scrapped. *Torquay* (F43) is a Navigation Training and Direction Trials ship and is about to be placed on the disposals list.

'Tribal' class
Type 81 Frigates (1958-64)
Ashanti   (F117)
Nubian   (F131)

Displacement: 2,340t
Arrangement: One 4.5in gun; hull plating rises under bridge and lattice mast, then drops under two funnels.
Notes: The 'Tribals' reversed the earlier trend of having separate types of frigate for specialist roles; the Type 81 combined anti-submarine, anti-aircraft and patrol functions in the one hull. *Ashanti* is used as a harbour training ship at Portsmouth, and *Nubian* is awaiting disposal. The others have been sold to other navies or for scrap.

'Salisbury' class
Type 61 Frigates (1952-60)
Salisbury   (F32)

Displacement: 2,210t
Arrangement: Forecastle curves down under twin 4.5in gun turret, then rises to bridge, before dropping to main deck level; two 'macks' (combined mast and funnel stacks); hull cut away aft.
Notes: The Type 61s were designed as specialised fighter-direction frigates: *Salisbury* is now a harbour training ship at Devonport.

Landing Ships, Tank
(1944-45)
Lofoten   (K07)   *Zeebrugge*   (L3532)

Stalker   (L3515)

Displacement: 2,130t
Arrangement: Bow doors; tank-deck; engines aft.
Notes: These vessels are awaiting disposal at Rosyth (*Lofoten* — which served for a time as a helicopter support ship — and *Stalker*) and at Plymouth (*Zeebrugge*).

'A' class
Type 21 Frigates (1969-78)

Amazon (F169)	*Ambuscade* (F172)	*Alacrity* (F174)
Active (F171)	*Arrow* (F173)	*Avenger* (F185)

Displacement: 2,030t
Dimensions: 117×12.7×3.7m
Arrangement: One 4.5in (114mm) Mk 8 gun in round mounting; deck rises one level here; four single Exocet anti-ship missile launchers; bridge with two 20mm guns on each side; the multi-barrel devices (mounted on each side of the superstructure of most warships) are chaff and decoy launchers for confusing enemy radar and missiles; array of dish aerials for GWS24 radar (including Orion RTN-10X) for gunnery and Seacat control (all Seacat control systems include optical sighting and guidance facilities); solid mast carrying thin, narrow aerial for Type 992 general purpose radar at masthead and smaller, similar aerial for Type 978 navigation radar on foretop; one set of triple 12.75in (324mm) anti-submarine torpedo tubes on each side of superstructure; tall thin mast; funnel venting two Olympus and two Tyne gas turbines (each set comprises one of each type, driving one propeller shaft; GWS24 radar aerial array; one quadruple Seacat missile launcher (to be replaced with Sea Wolf launcher); hull drops one level here; hangar and flight deck for one Westland Lynx Mk 2 or Wasp helicopter; hull cut away right aft.
Speed: 30kt
Complement: 175
Notes: The 'A' class is designed as a patrol frigate, intended for independent operation or in company with one or two of her sisterships and able to undertake a variety of hunting, escort and other tasks.

'H' class
Survey Ships (1964-74)

Hecate (A137)	*Hydra* (A144)
Hecla (A133)	

Improved 'H' class
Herald   (A138)

Displacement: 1,950-2,030t
Dimensions: 93.3×15×4.7m
Arrangement: White yacht-like appearance; hull has raised bulwark at bows; garage on forecastle for small vehicle; bridge; solid mast; buff funnel venting three diesel engines powering one electric motor which drives one

propeller shaft; hull drops one level amidships (run aft screened by bulwarks); hangar and flight-deck aft for one Westland Wasp helicopter.
Speed: 14kt
Complement: 118-128
Notes: All Royal Navy warships update the charts they carry and report new data and phenomena. But these specialist survey ships carry all the equipment necessary for mapping the world's oceans and the seabed. Nowadays, the latter is as significant as the delineation of the shore, deep-diving nuclear submarines having to know the exact location of undersea ridges and plains. Yet — apart from the detailed portrayal of defence installations — no such information is kept secret. Admiralty charts can be purchased by any intending seafarer of any nation, a contribution to safe travel and world civilisation of inestimable worth.

Hydra is due to be paid off when the new 1,000t survey ship *Roebuck* is commissioned at the end of 1985.

'Castle' class
Offshore Patrol Vessel (1979-82)
Dumbarton Castle   (P265)
Leeds Castle   (P258)

Displacement: 1,450t
Dimensions: 81×11.5×4.2m
Arrangement: Long sheering flush deck with raking stem and square stern; superstructure perched amidships on very bare hull; one 40mm gun; square bridge; solid mast.
Main engines: Two diesels, each driving one propeller shaft
Speed: 19kt
Complement: 50
Notes: The 'Castles' can operate a Sea King helicopter, lay mines or transport a 25-man Royal Marine raiding party.

'Abdiel'
Exercise Minelayer (1966-67)
Abdiel   (N21)

Displacement: 1,400t
Dimensions: 80.8×11.7×3.1m
Arrangement: One 40mm gun; square bridge with tripod mast; funnel venting two diesels, each driving one propeller shaft; crane and other mine-warfare equipment; square stern with two doors for laying a total of 44 mines.
Speed: 16kt
Complement: 98
Notes: *Abdiel* serves as a headquarters and depot ship for smaller mine counter-measures vessels. Although the mines she lays are dummy ones for MCMVs to practise finding and sweeping, she could also lay lethal munitions in an emergency. Her slow speed would not permit her to do this off an hostile shore, and so *Abdiel's* minefields would be defensive ones; guarding the approaches to important harbours and anchorages.

Top:
The Type 21 'A' class frigate HMS *Ardent* on patrol in the Gulf of Oman in 1981. A year later she had been sunk in the Falklands War.

Above:
A Sea King helicopter from 819 Squadron operating with the offshore patrol vessel HMS *Leeds Castle*.

Below:
The 'Hunt' class MCMV HMS *Middleton* at Portsmouth on 8 August 1984. The Administrative office block in the background is crowned by a reconstruction of the 19th century semaphore tower, itself topped by a tall mast. *Author*

'Blackwood' class
Type 14 Frigates (1953-58)
Russell (F97)

Displacement: 1,200t
Arrangement: Forecastle curves down, rises to form part of bridge, then drops two levels to main deck; tripod mast; funnel; small tripod mast; superstructure runs aft.
Notes: Built as anti-submarine escorts, but so specialised they could only fulfil this one function; they were also too slow to overhaul the latest nuclear submarines at speed under water, when the latter entered service. *Russell* is used for harbour training at Portsmouth.

'Island' class
Patrol Vessels (1975-79)

Alderney (P278)	*Jersey* (P295)	*Shetland* (P298)
Anglesey (P277)	*Lindisfarne* (P300)	
Guernsey (P297)	*Orkney* (P299)	

Displacement: 940t
Dimensions: 59.6 × 10.4 × 4.3m
Arrangement: Trawler-like appearance; raised forecastle; one 40mm gun on 'bandstand'; square bridge and superstructure with tripod mast and squat funnel (venting two diesels, together driving one propeller shaft).
Speed: 16kt
Complement: 34-40
Notes: Used for oil-rig protection.

Wakeful
Target Ship
Wakeful (A236)

Displacement: 910t
Dimensions: 38.9 × 10.7 × 4.8m
Arrangement: Tug-like appearance with raised forecastle, tripod mast, piled-up bridge and large squat funnel (venting two diesels).
Complement: 18
Notes: Purchased from Sweden in 1974, *Wakeful* serves as a target for submarines practising sonar techniques and exercising with dummy torpedoes in the Firth of Clyde. By being in company with submarines on such occasions and when they are passing through the Clyde, she can ensure that other ships are made aware of the presence of submarines, and thus mitigate the chances of collision or other accident. *Wakeful* may soon be replaced by *Northella* (see 'Harbour and Reserve Craft').

'Fawn' class
Coastal Survey Ships (1966-68)

Beagle (A319)	*Fawn* (A325)
Bulldog (A317)	*Fox* (A320)

Displacement: 810t
Dimensions: 57.6 × 11.4 × 3.7m
Arrangement: White yacht-like appearance, with piled-up bridge and superstructure (perhaps one 20mm gun on each side); mast; buff funnel venting four diesels, each pair driving one propeller shaft; hull plating drops in two stages amidships, with bulwarks on after deck.
Speed: 15kt
Complement: 38
Notes: Usually work in pairs on some overseas location. The survey launch *Gleaner* (A86) was commissioned on 12 December 1983 for operations in the Solent and around the Channel Islands. She measures 15 × 4.55 × 1.62m and has a crew of six.

'Hunt' class
Mine Counter-Measures Vessels (1975-)

Brecon (M29)	*Brocklesby* (M33)	*Chiddingfold* (M37)
Ledbury (M30)	*Middleton* (M34)	*Bicester* (M38)
Cattistock (M31)	*Dulverton* (M35)	*Hurworth* (M39)
Cottesmore (M32)	*Atherstone* (M36)	— (M40 ?)

Displacement: 625t
Dimensions: 60 × 9.9 × 2.2m
Arrangement: One 40mm gun; bridge with radar; solid mast with funnel venting two diesels, each driving one propeller shaft; glass-fibre reinforced plastic (GRP) hull drops one level here; sweep deck with equipment for lowering and streaming devices for dealing with all types of magnetic, acoustic and moored contact mines.
Speed: 16kt
Complement: 45
Notes: The 'Hunt' class combines in one hull the ability to find and then eliminate mines, two functions which had to be carried out in two different types of the 'Ton' class. The 'Hunt's' equipment includes high-definition sonar which enables the operator to locate precisely and then identify the type of mine laid in the area. If it is in such a position or of such a type that the ship cannot deal with it by steaming overhead and trailing a sweep astern, then a PAP 104 is launched. This is a French-built miniature submarine, which is remotely-controlled by wire-guidance, the operator watching a screen relaying a television picture from a camera in the PAP 104. Once alongside the suspicious object, it releases an explosive charge which in due time destroys the mine.

'River' class
Mine Counter-Measures Vessels (MCMVs)

Waveney (M2003)	*Blackwater* (M2007)	*Orwell* (M2011)
Carron (M2004)	*Itchen* (M2008)	*Ribble* (M2012)
Dovey (M2005)	*Helmsdale* (M2009)	*Spey* (M2013)
Helford (M2006)	*Humber* (M2010)	*Arun* (M2014)

Displacement: 810t-890t
Dimensions: 47.5 × 10.5 × 3.1m

Right:
The launch of the 'River' class MCMV HMS *Waveney*.

Below:
The minehunter HMS *Bossington* and the inshore survey vessel HMS *Woodlark* at Portsmouth on 6 June 1984. *Author*

Bottom:
The mooring, salvage and boom defence vessel RMAS *Goldeneye* in Portsmouth Harbour on 6 June 1984. *Author*

Arrangement: High trawler-like bow and general appearance; forecastle bulwarks; squarish bridge with solid pylon mast; two tall rectangular funnels side-by-side, each venting one diesel (each driving one propeller shaft; hull drops one level aft.

Notes: Inspired by the 'Venturer' class of stern trawlers, the 'Rivers' are equipped with Extra Deep Armed Team Sweeps (EDATS). Pairs of 'Rivers' stream one wire between them which follows the contours of the seabed as deep as 200m, detonating mines laid to catch British nuclear submarines passing to and from their patrol areas. These weapons are laid so deep that they are unlikely to be triggered by the minesweepers' own hulls, so the 'Rivers' have been built of steel, a cheaper but heavier material than the glass-fibre 'Hunts'. For their own safety in shallow water the 'Rivers' have enhanced degaussing protection.

'Peacock' class
Patrol Vessels (1982-85)

Peacock (P239)	*Starling* (P241)	*Swift* (P243)
Plover (P240)	*Swallow* (P242)	

Displacement: 710ft
Dimensions: 62.2 × 10 × 5.5m
Arrangement: Raking bow and flush deck; one round-turreted 76mm Oto Melara Compact gun mounting with range of 3nm; square bridge and superstructure with two 7.62mm machine guns on each side; light lattice mast; single funnel venting two diesels, each driving one propeller shaft.
Speed: 25kt
Complement: 42
Notes: For service at Hong Kong.

'Ton' class
Mine Counter-Measures Vessels (1951-60/73)

Minehunter/Sweeper
Wilton (M1116)
(Combines both roles in a 1973-hull of glass-reinforced plastic.)

Minehunters

Bildeston (M1110)	*Gavinton* (M1140)	*Maxton* (M1165)
Brinton (M1114)	*Hubberston* (M1147)	*Nurton* (M1166)
Bronington (M1115)	*Iveston* (M1151)	*Sheraton* (M1181)
Bossington (M1133)	*Kirkliston* (M1157)	

RNR minehunters (training ships)

Brereton (M1113) (Mersey)	*Kellington* (M1154) (Sussex)
Kedleston (M1153) (Forth)	

Minesweeper
Upton (M1187)

RNR minesweepers (training ships)

Alfriston (M1103) (Solent)	*Shavington* (M1180) (Ulster)
Cuxton (M1125) (Tay)	*Lewiston* (M1208) (London)
Hodgeston (M1146) (Clyde)	*Crofton* (M1216) (Tyne)

Offshore division fishery protection squadron

Bickington	(M1109)	*Walkerton*	(M1188)	*Stubbington*	(M1204)
Crichton	(M1124)	*Wotton*	(M1195)		
Pollington	(M1173)	*Soberton*	(M1200)		

(Based at Rosyth, each of these vessels carries an extra large searchlight to illuminate and identify craft fishing illegally in British territorial waters.)

Large patrol craft

Beachampton	(P1007)	*Wasperton*	(P1089)	*Yarnton*	(P1096)
Monkton	(P1055)	*Wolverton*	(P1093)		

(Formerly the 6th Patrol Squadron based at Hong Kong, they have been replaced by 'Peacock' class patrol vessels and will probably be placed on the disposals list.)

Displacement: 370-460t
Dimensions: 46.3×8.7×2.6m
Arrangement: One 40mm gun; square bridge; tripod mast; deck drops one level here, but run aft screened with bulwarks; funnel venting two diesels, each driving one propeller shaft; perhaps one 40mm or one 20mm gun on deckhouse aft; twin derricks for handling mine warfare equipment.
Speed: 15kt
Complement: 38
Notes: These are the survivors of over 100 'Ton' class vessels, plus *Glasserton* (M1141, harbour training ship) and *Laleston* (M1158, awaiting scrapping). As their type names imply, some of them specialise in locating mines by high-definition sonar and then despatching frogmen to deal with them underwater. The minesweepers stream equipment astern to cut mooring wires and detonate influence mines.

Both types of mine could be encountered in coastal waters. The mining of the approaches to ports could be the most effective method of forcing unpleasant terms on the British people in an international incident of limited objectives — a form of blackmail to which nuclear response would be an over-reaction. Eliminating the mines would be the only chance of survival without surrender; and for that a large force of MCMVs is required. Many of them are manned by part-time sailors of the Royal Naval Reserve. There have been suggestions that the growing complexity of mine warfare equipment may prove too complicated for personnel who do not spend all their time working with it. Such arguments have been used about non-regulars before, and they have always been disproved when an emergency has arisen. Indeed, the widespread introduction of electronic gadgetry throughout civilian life probably means that most people now have an enhanced manual and mental dexterity when it comes to assimilating the techniques of unfamiliar devices.

Single-Role Minehunters
Displacement: 460t
Dimensions: 50×9m
Arrangement: Fast attack craft hull with high square superstructure occupying most of length; squarish bridge; solid pylon mast; square funnel; venting two diesels, each driving one propeller shaft (also has bow thruster);

light crane aft for deploying variable-depth sonar and remote-control mine-disposal system.

'Bird' class
Large Patrol Craft (1974-77)

Cygnet (P261)	*Peterel* (P262)
Kingfisher (P260)	*Sandpiper* (P263)

Displacement: 130t (approx)
Dimensions: 36.6×6.6×2.7m (approx)
Arrangement: Large motor launches; one funnel venting two diesels, each driving one propeller shaft; derrick aft.
Speed: 18kt
Complement: 19
Notes: Two accompany the MCMVs at Rosyth, while *Peterel* and *Sandpiper* are attached to the RNC, Dartmouth.

Hovercraft and Hydrofoils
Although the Inter-Service Hovercraft Unit has now been disbanded, some hovercraft may still be seen awaiting disposal at their former base at Lee-on-Solent, where they were used to evaluate their suitability as MCMV's and assault craft.

VT2-type
No 001

Displacement: 100t
Arrangement: Very big streamlined craft, with control position offset to port, and two huge ducted-propeller nacelles right aft.

BH7 (Wellington)-type
P235

Displacement: 55t
Arrangement: Fairly bare roof which carries control position, four-bladed propeller on vertical fin, and two widely-spaced raking rudders.

SRN (Winchester)-type

Displacement: 10t
Arrangement: Passenger-carrying appearance to superstructure; two propellers and nacelles right aft.

SRN5-type
Displacement: 10t
Arrangement: Cluttered top to superstructure; propeller and twin-rudder unit right aft.

Speedy (*P296*)
Notes: Hydrofoil with fast attack craft hull; now awaiting disposal at Portsmouth.

Landing Craft Utility (LCU)
Formerly Landing Craft Mechanised Mk 9 (1963-66)

LCU700	LCU706	LCU711
LCU701	LCU707	LCU3507
LCU702	LCU708	LCU3508
LCU704	LCU709	
LCU705	LCU710	

Displacement: 76t
Dimensions: 26×6.6×1.7m
Arrangement: Bow ramp; well-deck for two tanks or 100t stores; wheelhouse aft.
Main engines: two diesels each driving one propeller.
Speed: 10kt
Complement: 8
Notes: LCUs are usually crewed by Royal Marines. Hulls often bear additional identification numbers prefixed with F (*Fearless*), T (*Intrepid*), and P (the Royal Marines Amphibious Unit at Poole).

The older LCM(7) is similar, but smaller. LCM7037 and LCM7100 have now been relegated to use as harbour craft only. Two LCM(9)s belong to the Army and are manned by the Royal Corps of Transport (RCT). Indeed, the Army operates a number of other types of landing craft, the largest with a displacement of almost 1,000t. They are all typical landing craft configuration, with bow ramp, tank deck, and engines and wheelhouse aft. They are all crewed by soldiers and the larger ones are capable of undertaking lengthy sea voyages. RCT landing craft often have those letters painted on their hulls and may be seen in the harbours of any area where the British Army is based or operating.

They are named after amphibious operations and rivers. All British landing craft — whether Navy or Army — are usually grey, although some may be given camouflage schemes appropriate to their current operational area. Other governmental and official maritime organisations own and maintain craft of naval appearance and function; for example, there are Royal Air Force air/sea rescue launches; HM Coastguard cutters; Trinity House pilot vessels; police launches; RNLI lifeboats; Sail Training Scheme vessels; Customs & Excise launches; and Scottish Home Department fishery protection vessels. Any of these may be seen in close proximity or actually in company with Royal Naval vessels in coastal waters. On occasions some may be taken temporarily into Naval service for some particular task.

'Dark' and 'Brave' class
Fast Attack Craft (1956-58)
Dark Hero (P1115)
Brave Borderer (P1011)

Displacement: 50-75ft
Arrangement: Traditional MTB hulls with minimum superstructure. They may show vestiges of either gun or torpedo armament.
Notes: Both are now awaiting scrapping, probably at Pembroke Dock.

Landing Craft Vehicle & Personnel

LCVP(1)	LCVP(2)	LCVP(3)
LCVP 102	LCVP 142	LCVP 150
LCVP 112	LCVP 143	LCVP 151
LCVP 118	LCVP 144	LCVP 152
LCVP 120	LCVP 145	LCVP 153
LCVP 123	LCVP 146	LCVP 154
LCVP 127	LCVP 147	LCVP 155
LCVP 128	LCVP 148	LCVP 156
LCVP 134	LCVP 149	LCVP 157
LCVP 136		LCVP 158

Displacement: 8.6t
Dimensions: 12.2-13.1×3×0.8m
Arrangement: Bow ramp; well deck for 35 troops or two small vehicles; engines and wheelhouse aft.
Main engines: Two diesels each driving one shaft.
Speed: 10kt
Complement: 3-4
Notes: A postwar development of a wartime design, the basic hull can be adapted for a variety of tasks during amphibious operations.

Landing Craft Personnel (Large) Mk 3 (1940s)

LCPL501	LCPL556
LCPL503	

Displacement: 6.6t
Dimensions: 11.2×3.4×1m
Arrangement: Small wooden craft, with more seaworthy bow, capable of carrrying 25 troops.
Main engines: Two diesels, each driving one propeller shaft
Speed: 12kt
Complement: 3
Notes: More suitable for raiding than other larger craft. They are now probably only used for training, having been superseded by rubber inflatables with paddles and outboard motors (for silent or high-speed work respectively).

Harbour & Reserve Craft

Newton
Trials ship (1973-76)
Newton (A367)

Displacement: 4,000t
Dimensions: 98.6×16.5×5.7m
Arrangement: Long flush-deck hull; cable-laying sheaves and pole mast at bow; bipod mast and derrick; massive superstructure and square bridge;

solid mast and two funnels side-by-side (venting three diesels together driving one propeller shaft); gallows at stern.
Speed: 16kt
Complement: 86
Notes: Used for sonar trials off Plymouth, with cable-laying as a secondary task.

Crystal
Trials Ship (1970-71)
Crystal   (RDV01)

Displacement: 3,090t
Dimensions: 126.1×17×1.7m
Arrangement: Looks like a long white factory, with a tall block of flats at one end, and an oil-rig at the other.
Complement: 60
Notes: Permanently based at Portland conducting experiments for the Admiralty Underwater Weapons Establishment. Can only be moved by tugs as she has no propulsion of her own.

'Whitehead' class
Trials Ships (1969)
Whitehead   (A364)

Displacement: 3,090t full load
Dimensions: 97.2×14.6×5.2m
Arrangement: Mast and derrick; superstructure, bridge (with mast) and funnel (venting two diesels together driving one propeller shaft) aft.
Speed: 15.5kt
Complement: 57
Notes: *Whitehead* has all the equipment required for preparing new weapons for test, carrying out the firing, tracking the weapon and target, and subsequently analysing the results. All trials ships are crewed by RMAS, accompanied by a number of appropriate scientists.

St Margarets
Cable Ship (1940-43)
St Margarets   (A259)

Displacement: 1,320t
Arrangement: Sheaves over clipper bow; superstructure, bridge and funnel located towards the stern.
Notes: Used for laying signal cables between RN bases, and now being prepared for disposal.

Seaforth Clansman
Diving Ship (1977)
Seaforth Clansman

Displacement: 1,200t deadweight
Dimensions: 78.6×14.1×5m
Arrangement: Like a huge tug; bulwarks forward topped by lofty helicopter platform; gallows mast; bridge and superstructure forward; mast and funnel (venting four diesels, each pair driving one propeller shaft); heavy crane aft.
Speed: 13kt
Notes: Chartered as an RFA in 1978. Originally based at Aberdeen for oil rig patrol. Carries firefighting and anti-pollution equipment, plus a diving team. Gear can be launched either over the stern ramp, or via a moonpool amidships. Now converted as Antarctic ice patrol ship and painted with red hull and buff-yellow upperworks.

'Ro' class
Ocean Tugs (1969-74)
Robust (A366)   *Roysterer* (A361)
Rollicker (A502)

Displacement: 1,660t full load
Dimensions: 54.7×11.7×5.5m
Arrangement: Large bridge; one solid mast and two 'macks' (combined mast and funnel stacks, each venting one diesel, each driving one propeller shaft) forming a tripod structure with firefighting platform; pole mast and derrick.
Speed: 15kt
Complement: 41
Notes: These tugs can carry out tows from one side of the ocean to the other. Yet when not required on such lengthy tasks, they can also undertake general work within the confines of dockyards and harbours. Their most dramatic role is that of rescue tug, for which they are provided with pumps, firefighting nozzles and other specialised equipment.

Northella
Trawler
Northella

Displacement: 1,220t
Notes: Hired by the Navy to serve as a local escort for ships in home waters, accompanying nuclear submarines under way in the Clyde, for example. At other times she will provide seagoing experience for officers under training, perhaps visiting Dartmouth on such occasions. *Northella* is manned by a civilian crew.

Auricula
Trials Ship (1978-80)
Auricula (A285)

Displacement: 1,120t
Dimensions: 52×11×3.6m

Arrangement: Trawler-like vessel with high forecastle, square bridge; funnel (venting two diesels, each driving one propeller shaft); stern gallows.
Speed: 12kt
Complement: 32
Notes: Sonar trials at Portland

'Wild Duck' class
Mooring, Salvage and Boom Defence Vessels (1963-73)

Garganey (P194)	*Goldeneye* (P195)	*Goosander* (P196)
Mandarin (P192)	*Pintail* (P193)	*Pochard* (P197)

Displacement: 970-1,140t
Dimensions: 55.5/60.4×12.2×3.5m
Arrangement: Horns and rollers, mast and derrick; superstructure and bridge; funnel venting diesel driving one propeller shaft; pole mast.
Speed: 10kt
Complement: 24-32
Notes: Capable of handling buoys, laying moorings, dealing with booms and nets for protecting harbours and anchorages, and undertaking salvage work. Manned by the Royal Maritime Auxiliary Service (RMAS).

'Kin' class
Mooring, Salvage and Boom Defence Vessels (1942-45)

Kinbrace (A281)	*Kinloss* (A482)
Kingarth (A232)	*Uplifter* (A507)

Displacement: 970t
Dimensions: 51.9×10.8×2.9m
Arrangement: Horns and rollers over bow; goalpost mast and derricks; piled-up superstructure and bridge; funnel venting diesel driving one propeller shaft; tall pole mast; gantry.
Speed: 9kt
Complement: 34
Notes: Manned by RMAS for salvage, boom defence and mooring work. The three 'Kins' are due for disposal, and will be replaced by *Salmaster*, *Salmoor* and *Salmaid* now under construction.

'Magnet' class
Degaussing Vessels (1978-80)

Magnet (A114)
Lodestone (A115)

Displacement: 970t full load
Arrangement: Foremast; hull plating raised amidships; square bridge and superstructure, with twin funnels (each venting one diesel).
Speed: 12kt
Complement: 15
Notes: Carry electric equipment to reduce or alter a ship's magnetic signature, thus lessening her chances of triggering a magnetic mine.

'Kinterbury' class
Armament Carriers (1976-77)
Kinterbury (A378)
Throsk (A379)

Displacement: 830t
Dimensions: 70.5×11.9×4.6m
Arrangement: Traditional coaster appearance; forecastle; mast and derrick; raised poop with bridge, goalpost mast and square funnel (venting two diesels, together driving one propeller shaft).
Notes: Used for carrying 1,170t of guns, launchers, missiles, ammunition and other explosive stores and ordnance, between bases.

'Typhoon'
Ocean Tug (1958-60)
Typhoon (A95)

Displacement: 810t
Dimensions: 61×12.2×4m
Arrangement: High bow; pole mast; bridge; funnel venting two diesels together driving one propeller shaft; tripod mast.
Speed: 16kt
Notes: The Navy's ocean tugs are operated by the RMAS. They often spend time based at Gibraltar or other strategic locations, standing-by to proceed to the assistance of RN vessels in distress.

'Con' class
Ocean Tugs (1955-59)
Confident (A290)   *Advice* (A89)
Accord (A90)   *Agile* (A88)

Displacement: 770t full load
Dimensions: 49.3×10.7×3.4m
Arrangement: Round bow; square bridge; tripod mast; funnel venting four diesels, each pair driving one propeller shaft; pole mast.
Speed: 13kt
Complement: 42
Notes: The complement of ocean tugs normally includes a naval salvage party to board the casualty for damage control and handling towing lines. These 'Con' class tugs are due to be replaced by Twin Unit Tractor Tugs now under construction.

'Tornado' class
Torpedo Recovery Vessels (1977-80)
Tornado (A140)   *Tormentor* (A142)
Torch (A141)   *Toreador* (A143)

Displacement: 698t full load
Dimensions: 40×9.2×3.3m

Arrangement: Tug-like hull; square bridge; two funnels side-by-side (each venting one diesel); forecastle deck ends here.
Speed: 14kt
Complement: 17
Notes: Recover torpedoes over the stern after exercises by frigates and submarines, etc.

Dolwen
Fleet Tender (1962)
Dolwen

Displacement: 610t full load
Dimensions: 41.1×9×4.4m
Arrangement: Tug-like hull with bridge, mast and funnel (venting diesel driving one propeller shaft) right forward; gallows aft.
Notes: Based at Aberforth as range safety ship.

'Torrid' class
Torpedo Recovery Vessels (1970-72)
Torrent   (A127)
Torrid   (A128)

Displacement: 560grt
Dimensions: 46×9.6×3.4m
Arrangement: Raised forecastle right forward, with mast and derrick at break of forecastle; piled-up superstructure with bridge, light mast and funnel (venting diesels); crane over stern well for torpedo recovery.
Speed: 12kt
Complement: 19
Notes: RMAS vessels specially designed for recovery of torpedoes after exercises and trials, a total of 32 being carried.

'Adept' class
Tugs (1979-)

Adept (A224)	*Careful* (A227)	*Nimble* (A222)
Bustler (A225)	*Forceful* (A221)	*Faithful* (A228)
Capable (A226)	*Powerful* (A223)	*Dexterous* (A231)

Displacement: 460t
Dimensions: 38.8×9.4×3.4m
Arrangement: Hexagonal bridge structure with light mast; two funnels side-by-side (each venting one diesel driving a Voith-Schneider propeller).
Speed: 12kt
Notes: Officially designated TUTS — or Twin-Unit (water) Tractors — they can undertake both coastal tows and complicated manoeuvres in restricted waters.

'Water' class
Carriers (1965-78)

Waterfall (Y17)	*Waterspout* (Y19)	*Waterman* (A146)
Watershed (Y18)	*Watercourse* (Y30)	
Waterside (Y20)	*Waterfowl* (Y31)	

Displacement: 290grt
Dimensions: 40.1×7.5×2.4m
Arrangement: Small raised forecastle; well-deck with pumping equipment; pole mast; raised poop with bridge.
Main engines: One diesel driving one propeller shaft.
Speed: 11kt
Complement: 11
Notes: Supply drinking and boiler feed water to warships. Smaller in size and fewer in number than previous classes of water carriers. Modern warships have very efficient distilling equipment and as fewer use boilers in their engine rooms, the need for pure water is therefore reduced. If necessary, arrangements could be made with local suppliers of this commodity, instead of having to maintain such vessels at remote harbours as was the former practice. It has been reported that the old water carrier *Freshspring* may be undergoing preservation in Bristol.

'Oil' class
Coastal Tankers (1967-70)

Oilbird (Y25)	*Oilman* (Y26)	*Oilstone* (Y22)
Oilfield (Y24)	*Oilpress* (Y21)	*Oilwell* (Y23)

Displacement: 280t
Dimensions: 42.5×9.1×2.5m
Arrangement: Superstructure, bridge and engines aft.
Main engines: Diesel driving one propeller shaft.
Speed: 10kt
Complement: 11
Notes: Operated by the RMAS, these vessels move some 250t of diesel or fuel oil from principal to subsidiary depots.

'Bullseye' class
Target Vessels (1961)

Bullseye	*Targe*
Magpie	

Displacement: 273grt
Dimensions: 35.9×7.7×3.7m
Arrangement: Trawler-hull with raised forecastle and poop; many strange-looking aerials on forecastle, foremast and welldeck (presumably duplications in case several are damaged); bridge and funnel (venting diesel) aft.
Speed: 12kt
Complement: 2

Notes: The passage crew disembark before these craft begin work as radio-controlled target vessels for live weaponry off Portland.

'Insect' class
Fleet Tenders (1970-73)

Bee (A216)	*Cricket* (A229)	*Scarab* (A272)
Cicala (A263)	*Gnat* (A239)	
Cockchafer (A230)	*Ladybird* (A253)	

Displacement: 250t
Dimensions: 34.1×8.5×3.4m
Arrangement: Look like small coasters; round bows; pole mast forward; raised poop with bridge and funnel (venting diesels driving one propeller shaft).
Speed: 10.5kt
Complement: 10
Notes: Some are fitted as store carriers (with a capacity of 200t) while others are armament carriers or mooring vessels, with resulting variations in craneage.

'E' class
Inshore Survey Craft (1957-58)

Echo (A70)	*Enterprise* (A71)
Egeria (A72)	

Displacement: 125t
Arrangement: The three vessels have been paid off and are probably awaiting scrapping. They were specially designed and built as inshore survey craft. They have a larger superstructure containing appropriate equipment and are usually painted white; but otherwise the 'E' class is virtually identical to the 'Ham' and 'Ley' classes of minecraft (approximately 32.5×6.7×1.7m). *Waterwitch* (M2270) and *Woodlark* (M2780) of that class were adapted as inshore survey craft. *Portisham* (M2781) and *Shipham* (M2726) are used for training by the Royal Naval Auxiliary Service at Portsmouth and Portland respectively. *Sandringham* (M2791) had an extended deckhouse as personnel transport on the Clyde. *Dittisham* (M2621), *Pagham* (M2716), *Flintham* (M2628), *Birdham* (M2785), *Odiham* (M2783), *Puttenham* (M2784), *Aveley* (M2002), *Thornham* (M2793) and *Thatcham* (M2790) and some other 'Hams' are all awaiting scrapping. All the survivors will soon be phased out of service.

They all have a fast attack craft hull with single deckhouse of varying length, a mast (usually lattice, but sometimes tripod) and assorted equipment aft. Diesel engines drive two propeller shafts.
Speed: 13kt
Complement: 15-18

Right:
The RMAS fleet tender RMAS *Dornoch* in the Firth of Forth on 19 May 1979.
A. Denholm

'Dog' class
Harbour Berthing Tugs

Alsatian (A106)	Deerhound (A155)	Pointer (A188)
Basset (A327)	Elkhound (A162)	Saluki (A182)
Cairn (A126)	Foxhound (A326)	Sealyham (A197)
Collie (A328)	Husky (A178)	Setter (A189)
Corgi (A330)	Labrador (A168)	Sheepdog (A250)
Dalmatian (A129)	Mastiff (A180)	Spaniel (A201)

Displacement: 170t full load
Dimensions: 28.7×7.5×3.7m
Arrangement: Raking bridge and light mast; two thin funnels side-by-side venting diesels.
Speed: 10kt
Complement: 8
Notes: All harbour berthing tugs are operated by the RMAS. Some are stationed at overseas bases like Gibraltar.

'Clovelly' Class
Fleet Tenders (1968-78)

Clovelly (A389)	Elsing (A277)
Criccieth (A391)	Epworth (A355)
Cricklade (A381)	Ettrick (A274)
Cromarty (A488)	Felstead (A348)
Denmead (A363)	Fintry (A394)
Dornoch (A490)	Fotherby (A341)
Dunster (A393)	Froxfield (A354)
Elkstone (A353)	Fulbeck (A365)

Glencoe   (A392)
Grasmere   (A402)
Hambledon   (A1769)
Harlech   (A1768)
Headcorn   (A1776)
Hever   (A1767)
Holmwood   (A1772)
Horning   (A1773)
Lamlash   (A208)
Lechlade   (A211)
Llandovery   (A207)
Vigilant   (A382)
Alert   (A510)
Loyal Mediator   (A161)
Loyal Moderator   (A220)

Loyal Volunteer   (A160)
Loyal Chancellor   (A1770)
Loyal Watcher   (A159)
Loyal Proctor   (A1771)
Loyal Helper   (A151)
Supporter   (A158)
Manly   (A92)
Melton   (A83)
Mentor   (A94)
Milbrook   (A97)
Messina   (A107)
Milford   (A81)
Menai   (A84)
Meon   (A87)

Diving Tenders
Ilchester   (A308)
Instow   (A309)
Invergordon   (A311)
Ironbridge   (A310)
Ilworth   (A318)
Datchet   (A357)

Displacement: 110t
Dimensions: 24.4×6.4×2m
Arrangement: Hull has rounded appearance; derrick and modernistic superstructure aft, plus funnel venting diesel driving one propeller shaft.

Datchet (based at Plymouth) is quite different; almost a fast attack craft hull, with raised forecastle and superstructure (no funnel) right forward.
Speed: 10.5-12kt
Complement: 5
Notes: These craft carry up to 200 standing passengers or 36t of cargo between ship and shore, operate regular ferry services around dockyards, and act as mobile bases for small working parties in restricted waters. Those fitted as diving tenders carry decompression chambers and other specialised equipment.

Most are manned by the Royal Maritime Auxiliary Service. Those patrolling off Northern Ireland, wear the White Ensign. Some are used by the Royal Naval Auxiliary Service, training part-time and reservist personnel for RFAs and the RMAS. Usually to be seen in British harbours, but several are stationed overseas. The Ms serve in the Royal Navy's Inshore Training Squadron.

'Aberdovey' class
Fleet Tenders (1963-71)

Abinger (Y11)	Beaulieu (A99)	Brodick (A105)
Alness (Y12)	Beddgelert (A100)	Cartmel (A350)
Alnmouth (Y13)	Bembridge (A101)	Cawsand (A351)
Appleby (A383)	Bibury (A103)	
Ashcott (Y16)	Blakeney (A104)	

Displacement: 90t
Dimensions: 24.2×5.5×1.7m
Arrangement: Like small coasters; raked stem; raised forecastle with pole mast at beginning of well-deck; raised poop with bridge, light mast and squat funnel (venting diesel driving one propeller shaft).
Speed: 10.5kt
Complement: 6
Notes: Can carry 25t of stores. Two of the home-based ones are used by the Sea Cadet Corps.

Endeavour
Torpedo Recovery Vessel (1966)
Endeavour　(A213)

Displacement: 90t
Dimensions: 23.2×4.4×3m
Arrangement: Tug-like hull with piled-up superstructure and funnel (venting one diesel driving one propeller shaft).
Speed: 10.5kt
Notes: Based at Portland; also acts as range safety craft.

'Girl' class
Harbour Berthing Tugs (1962-74)

Charlotte　(A210)	*Daphne*　(A156)	*Edith*　(A177)
Christine　(A217)	*Doris*　(A252)	
Daisy　(A145)	*Dorothy*　(A173)	

(Square bridge set well forward; two thin funnels, side-by-side.)

Felicity　(A112)	*Frances*　(A147)	*Gwendoline*　(A196)
Fiona　(A148)	*Genevieve*　(A150)	*Helen*　(A198)
Florence　(A149)	*Georgina*　(A152)	

(Modernistic superstructure set well aft; prominent guard rails with squat or curving funnel.)

Irene　(A181)	*Kathleen*　(A166)	*Mary*　(A175)
Isabel　(A183)	*Kitty*　(A170)	*Myrtle*　(A199)
Joan　(A190)	*Lesley*　(A172)	*Nancy*　(A202)
Joyce　(A193)	*Lila*　(A174)	*Norah*　(A205)

(Small wheelhouse set amidships with funnel almost hidden.)

Displacement: 40-110t
Dimensions: 177.7 maximum length
Speed: 8-10kt
Notes: All diesel-driven, these vessels have Voith-Schneider vertical propellers and are so manoeuvrable that they are sometimes called 'water tractors'. At one time the sub-types were rather whimsically known as 'Girls', 'Modified Girls', 'Improved Girls' and 'Supergirls', but nowadays they are usually referred to by the lead ship of each class.

'Tracker' class
University Training Craft (1982-84)

Attacker (P281)   *Hunter* (P284)   *Striker* (P285)
Fencer (P283)   *Chaser* (P282)

Displacement: 30t
Dimensions: 19.3×5×1.5m
Arrangement: Fast attack craft hull and superstructure.
Main engines: Two diesels, each driving one propeller shaft
Speed: 29kt
Notes: Attached to RNR divisions. Projected vessels may be named *Archer*, *Biter*, *Smiter*, *Pursuer*, *Blazer*, *Dasher*, *Charger*, *Ranger* and *Trumpeter*.

'RTTL' Type
Torpedo Recovery Vessels
L72
Osprey
Redpole (P259)

Displacement: 30-35t
Arrangement: Ex-RAF rescue and target-towing launches, with simple superstructure, mast and derrick; hull cut-away aft.
Notes: Based on the Clyde.

Miscellaneous Vessels

These include;

Endsleigh
(Based at Rosyth carrying out trials for the Admiralty Marine Technology Establishment.)

STVO2
(Shock trials vessel for experiments assessing the damage caused by nearmiss explosions.)

Oliver Twist
Smike
Uriah Heap
(20t RNR launches.)

'James Bond' FDC7001
(Unofficial name for Faslane personnel transport.)

There are also the floating docks AFD26, AFD58, AFD59 and AFD60.

General Notes

Pennant numbers are not always painted on submarines (which sometimes display a nameboard when entering or leaving harbour), and are not always painted on Royal Fleet Auxiliaries or Royal Marine Auxiliary Service craft.

Both RFAs and RMAS vessels have their names permanently displayed on either side of the bow and on their counter.

The names of Royal Navy warships are usually displayed in permanent raised letters or on a nameboard, sometimes on either side of the superstructure and sometimes on either side of the hull — but always towards the stern.

Other combinations of letters and figures denote the squadron to which the vessel belongs, and sometimes her place in it. These can be displayed almost anywhere, including on the funnel.

No pennant numbers or other markings are displayed by Her Majesty's Yacht *Britannia*.

(b)   building (may now be complete)
(m)   preserved or museum ship
(n)   unofficial
(s)   used as stationary harbour accommodation, or store or training ship; or due for disposal, probably for scrap (which may already have been done), or likely to be so assigned in the near future.
(u)   unnamed

A00	*Britannia*	A103	*Bibury*
A70	*Echo* (s)	A104	*Blakeney*
A71	*Enterprise* (s)	A105	*Brodick*
A72	*Egeria* (s)	A106	*Alsatian*
A75	*Tidespring*	A107	*Messina*
A77	*Pearleaf*	A109	*Bayleaf*
A78	*Plumleaf*	A112	*Felicity*
A79	*Appleleaf*	A114	*Magnet*
A81	*Brambleleaf*	A115	*Lodestone*
A83	*Melton*	A122	*Olwen*
A84	*Menai*	A123	*Olna*
A86	*Gleaner*	A124	*Olmeda*
A87	*Meon*	A126	*Cairn*
A88	*Agile*	A127	*Torrent*
A89	*Advice*	A128	*Torrid*
A90	*Accord*	A129	*Dalmatian*
A91	*Milford*	A131	*Reliant*
A92	*Manly*	A133	*Hecla*
A94	*Mentor*	A134	*Rame Head* (s)
A95	*Typhoon*	A137	*Hecate*
A97	*Milbrook*	A138	*Herald*
A99	*Beaulieu*	A140	*Tornado*
A100	*Beddgelert*	A141	*Torch*
A101	*Bembridge*	A142	*Tormentor*

A143	Toreador	A222	Nimble
A144	Hydra	A223	Powerful
A145	Daisy	A224	Adept
A146	Waterman	A225	Bustler
A147	Frances	A226	Capable
A148	Fiona	A227	Careful
A149	Florence	A228	Faithful
A150	Genevieve	A229	Cricket
A152	Georgina	A230	Cockchafer
A155	Deerhound	A231	Dexterous
A156	Daphne	A232	Kingarth (s)
A157	Loyal Helper	A236	Wakeful
A158	Supporter	A239	Gnat
A159	Loyal Watcher	A250	Sheepdog
A160	Loyal Volunteer	A252	Doris
A161	Loyal Mediator	A253	Ladybird
A162	Elkhound	A259	St Margarets (s)
A166	Kathleen	A263	Cicala
A168	Labrador	A268	Green Rover
A170	Kitty	A269	Grey Rover
A171	Endurance	A270	Blue Rover
A172	Lesley	A271	Gold Rover
A173	Dorothy	A272	Scarab
A174	Lila	A273	Black Rover
A175	Mary	A274	Ettrick
A177	Edith	A277	Elsing
A178	Husky	A281	Kinbrace (s)
A180	Mastiff	A285	Auricula
A181	Irene	A290	Confident
A182	Saluki	A308	Ilchester
A183	Isabel	A309	Instow
A188	Pointer	A310	Ironbridge
A189	Setter	A311	Invergordon
A190	Joan	A317	Bulldog
A191	Berry Head (s)	A318	Ixworth
A193	Joyce	A319	Beagle
A196	Gwendoline	A320	Fox
A187	Sealyham	A325	Fawn
A198	Helen	A326	Foxhound
A199	Myrtle	A327	Basset
A201	Spaniel	A328	Collie
A202	Nancy	A330	Corgi
A205	Norah	A341	Fotherby
A207	Llandovery	A348	Felsted
A208	Lamlash	A350	Cartmel
A210	Charlotte	A351	Cawsand
A211	Lechlade	A353	Elkstone
A213	Endeavour	A354	Froxfield
A216	Bee	A355	Epworth
A217	Christine	A357	Datchet
A220	Loyal Moderator	A361	Roysterer
A221	Forceful	A363	Denmead

A364	*Whitehead*	D91	*Nottingham*
A365	*Fulbeck*	D92	*Liverpool*
A366	*Robust*	D95	*Manchester*
A367	*Newton*	D96	*Gloucester*
A378	*Kinterbury*	D97	*Edinburgh*
A379	*Throsk*	D98	*York*
A381	*Cricklade*	D108	*Cardiff*
A382	*Vigilant*		
A383	*Appleby*	F10	*Aurora*
A385	*Fort Grange*	F12	*Achilles*
A386	*Fort Austin*	F15	*Euryalus*
A389	*Clovelly*	F16	*Diomede*
A391	*Criccieth*	F18	*Galatea*
A392	*Glencoe*	F28	*Cleopatra*
A393	*Dunster*	F32	*Salisbury* (s)
A394	*Fintry*	F38	*Arethusa*
A402	*Grasmere*	F39	*Naiad*
A480	*Resource*	F40	*Sirius*
A482	*Kinloss* (s)	F42	*Phoebe*
A486	*Regent*	F43	*Torquay* (s)
A488	*Cromarty*	F45	*Minerva*
A490	*Dornoch*	F47	*Danae*
A502	*Rollicker*	F52	*Juno*
A507	*Uplifter*	F56	*Argonaut*
A510	*Alert*	F57	*Andromeda*
A1767	*Hever*	F58	*Hermione*
A1768	*Harlech*	F60	*Jupiter*
A1769	*Hambledon*	F70	*Apollo*
A1770	*Loyal Chancellor*	F71	*Scylla*
A1771	*Loyal Proctor*	F72	*Ariadne*
A1772	*Holmwood*	F73	*Eastbourne* (s)
A1773	*Horning*	F75	*Charybdis*
A1776	*Headcorn*	F88	*Broadsword*
		F89	*Battleaxe*
AFD26	(u — floating dock)	F90	*Brilliant*
AFD58	(u — floating dock)	F91	*Brazen*
AFD59	(u — floating dock)	F92	*Boxer*
AFD60	(u — floating dock	F93	*Beaver* (b)
		F94	*Brave* (b)
C20	*Tiger* (s)	F95	*London* (b)
C35	*Belfast* (m)	F96	*Sheffield* (b)
		F97	*Russell* (s)
D12	*Kent* (s)	F101	*Yarmouth*
D19	*Glamorgan*	F103	*Lowestoft*
D20	*Fife*	F106	*Brighton* (s)
D23	*Bristol*	F107	*Rothesay*
D73	*Cavalier* (m)	F108	*Londonderry*
D86	*Birmingham*	F109	*Leander*
D87	*Newcastle*	F113	*Falmouth*
D88	*Glasgow*	F114	*Ajax*
D89	*Exeter*	F115	*Berwick*
D90	*Southampton*	F117	*Ashanti* (s)

F126	*Plymouth*	L701	(u — landing craft utility)
F127	*Penelope*	L702	(u — landing craft utility)
F129	*Rhyl*	L704	(u — landing craft utility)
F131	*Nubian* (s)	L705	(u — landing craft utility)
F169	*Amazon*	L706	(u — landing craft utility)
F171	*Active*	L707	(u — landing craft utility)
F172	*Ambuscade*	L708	(u — landing craft utility)
F173	*Arrow*	L709	(u — landing craft utility)
F174	*Alacrity*	L710	(u — landing craft utility)
F185	*Avenger*	L711	(u — landing craft utility)
		L3004	*Sir Bedivere*
FDC7001	*'James Bond'* (n)	L3027	*Sir Geraint*
		L3029	*Sir Lancelot*
K07	*Challenger*	L3036	*Sir Percivale*
K07	*Lofoten* (s)	L3505	*Sir Tristram*
K08	*Engadine*	L3507	(u — landing craft utility)
		L3508	(u — landing craft utility)
L10	*Fearless*	L3515	*Stalker* (s)
L11	*Intrepid*	L3522	*Sir Caradoc*
L72	(u — torpedo recovery vessel)	L3532	*Sir Lamorack*
L700	(u — landing craft utility)	L3532	*Zeebrugge* (s)

LCPL 501   (u — landing craft, personnel, large)
LCPL 503   (u — landing craft personnel, large)
LCPL 556   (u — landing craft personnel, large)
LCVP 102   (u — landing craft vehicle and personnel)
LCVP 112   (u — landing craft vehicle personnel)
LCVP 118   (u — landing craft vehicle and personnel)
LCVP 120   (u — landing craft vehicle and personnel)
LCVP 123   (u — landing craft vehicle and personnel)
LCVP 127   (u — landing craft vehicle and personnel)
LCVP 128   (u — landing craft vehicle and personnel)
LCVP 134   (u — landing craft vehicle and personnel)
LCVP 136   (u — landing craft vehicle and personnel)
LCVP 142   (u — landing craft vehicle and personnel)
LCVP 143   (u — landing craft vehicle and personnel)
LCVP 144   (u — landing craft vehicle and personnel)
LCVP 145   (u — landing craft vehicle and personnel)
LCVP 146   (u — landing craft vehicle and personnel)
LCVP 147   (u — landing craft vehicle and personnel)
LCVP 148   (u — landing craft vehicle and personnel)
LCVP 149   (u — landing craft vehicle and personnel)
LCVP 150   (u — landing craft vehicle and personnel)
LCVP 151   (u — landing craft vehicle and personnel)
LCVP 152   (u — landing craft vehicle and personnel)
LCVP 153   (u — landing craft vehicle and personnel)
LCVP 154   (u — landing craft vehicle and personnel)
LCVP 155   (u — landing craft vehicle and personnel)
LCVP 156   (u — landing craft vehicle and personnel)
LCVP 157   (u — landing craft vehicle and personnel)
LCVP 158   (u — landing craft vehicle and personnel)

M29	Brecon	M2011	Orwell
M30	Ledbury	M2012	Ribble
M31	Cattistock	M2013	Spey
M32	Cottesmore	M2014	Arun
M33	Brocklesby	M2270	Waterwitch
M34	Middleton	M2621	Dittisham (s)
M35	Dulverton	M2628	Flintham (s)
M36	Atherstone	M2716	Pagham (s)
M37	Chiddingfold	M2726	Shipham (s)
M38	Bicester	M2780	Woodlark (s)
M39	Hurworth	M2781	Portisham (s)
M40	(u — b)	M2783	Odiham (s)
M1103	Alfriston	M2784	Puttenham (s)
M1109	Bickington	M2785	Birdham (s)
M1110	Bildeston	M2790	Thatcham (s)
M1113	Brereton	M2791	Sandringham
M1114	Brinton	M2793	Thornham (s)
M1115	Bronington	N21	Abdiel
M1116	Wilton	P192	Mandarin
M1124	Crichton	P193	Pintail
M1125	Cuxton	P194	Garganey
M1133	Bossington	P195	Goldeneye
M1140	Gavinton	P196	Goosander
M1141	Glasserton (s)	P197	Pochard
M1146	Hodgeston	P235	(u — hovercraft — s)
M1147	Hubberston	P239	Peacock
M1151	Iveston	P240	Plover
M1153	Kedleston	P241	Starling
M1154	Kellington	P242	Swallow
M1157	Kirkliston	P243	Swift
M1158	Laleston (s)	P244	Protector
M1165	Maxton	P245	Guardian
M1166	Nurton	P246	Sentinel
M1173	Pollington	P258	Leeds Castle
M1180	Shavington	P259	Redpole
M1181	Sheraton	P260	Kingfisher
M1187	Upton	P261	Cygnet
M1188	Walkerton	P262	Peterel
M1195	Wotton	P263	Sandpiper
M1200	Soberton	P265	Dumbarton Castle
M1204	Stubbington	P277	Anglesey
M1208	Lewiston	P278	Alderney
M1216	Crofton	P281	Attacker
M2002	Waveley (s)	P282	Chaser
M2003	Waveney	P283	Fencer
M2004	Carron	P284	Hunter
M2005	Dovey	P285	Striker
M2006	Helford	P295	Jersey
M2007	Blackwater	P296	Speedy (s)
M2008	Itchen	P297	Guernsey
M2009	Helmsdale	P298	Shetland
M2010	Humber	P299	Orkney

P300	Lindisfarne
P1007	Beachampton (s)
P1011	Brave Borderer (s)
P1055	Monkton (s)
P1089	Wasperton (s)
P1093	Wolverton (s)
P1096	Yarnton (s)
P1115	Dark Hero (s)

R05	Invincible
R06	Illustrious
R07	Ark Royal
R12	Hermes
RDV 01	Crystal

S01	Porpoise (s)
S05	Finwhale (s)
S07	Sealion
S08	Walrus
S09	Oberon
S10	Odin
S11	Orpheus
S12	Olympus
S13	Osiris
S14	Onslaught
S15	Otter
S16	Oracle
S17	Ocelot
S18	Otus
S19	Opossum
S20	Opportune
S21	Onyx
S22	Resolution
S23	Repulse
S26	Renown
S27	Revenge
S46	Churchill

S48	Conqueror
S50	Courageous
S101	Dreadnought (s)
S102	Valiant
S103	Warspite
S104	Sceptre
S105	Spartan
S106	Splendid
S107	Trafalgar
S108	Sovereign
S109	Superb
S110	Turbulent
S115	Trenchant (b)
S117	Tireless (b)
S118	Torbay (b)
S126	Swiftsure
STV02	(u — shock trials vessel)

Y11	Abinger
Y12	Alness
Y13	Alnmouth
Y16	Ashcott
Y17	Waterfall
Y18	Watershed
Y19	Waterspout
Y20	Waterside
Y21	Oilpress
Y22	Oilstone
Y23	Oilwell
Y24	Oilfield
Y25	Oilbird
Y26	Oilman
Y30	Watercourse
Y31	Waterfowl

| No 001 | (u — hovercraft — s) |

Helicopters

Westland EH101

This helicopter is being developed jointly by Westland of Yeovil and Agusta of Italy. It is still at the design stage and should enter Fleet Air Arm service in the 1990s.

Arrangement: Streamlined fuselage with fully-retractable undercarriage; stepped cockpit and accommodation for crew of three/four; above and behind will be two intakes for two gas-turbines together driving a three/four-bladed main rotor; the tail unit will incorporate a fin and tailplane of fixed-wing appearance, plus a two/three-bladed tail-rotor; there will be a chin radome and sponsons for Stingray torpedoes and other anti-submarine weaponry.

Weight loaded: 14t
Speed: 172kt
Range: 1,100nm

Westland Sea King

The American Sikorsky S-61 first flew in 1959. Like a number of that company's previous designs, it became the subject of an agreement between Sikorsky and Westland, whereby the British firm built the machine under licence, but according to RN requirements. The first of these Sea Kings flew in 1969. Three versions are currently in sevice, totalling 94 machines.

The HAS Mk 5 is an anti-submarine helicopter, operational with 819 (Prestwick), 820 (*Invincible*), 814 (*Illustrious*), 824 (RFAs) and 826 Squadrons. Those with 706 Squadron are used for aircrew training at Culdrose.

The crew of four can employ radar to search the surface of the sea, or lower a sonar device to track underwater targets — a procedure known as 'dunking'. Markers can be dropped, followed by four Mk 11 depth-charges or four Mk 46 homing torpedoes. These latter are being replaced by the new Stingray torpedo. All these stores are carried externally.

The Sea King Mk 4 is an assault helicopter delivering 28 commandos, and is in service with 846 Squadron at Yeovilton. These machines are painted in military brown colours. Some Mk 2 Sea Kings have been fitted with Searchwater radar in inverted 'kettledrum' side-mounted radomes to serve as airborne early warning aircraft.

Both the Mk 5 and the Mk 4 can be used as search and rescue helicopters, and for vertical replenishment of ships at sea. This is the primary role of those Sea Kings carried aboard RFAs, although they can also augment the anti-submarine screen around the force during such a vulnerable operation as refuelling.

The Sea King fuselage has the appearance of a flying-boat hull, and can alight on a calm sea in an emergency. The main wheels disappear into two float-like sponsons, but the tail-wheel (at the end of the 'step') is non-retractable. The pilots sit high up. Just behind them are the intakes for the two Rolls-Royce Gnome gas-turbines, the entire powerplant being concealed within a long streamlined housing, which also supports the five-bladed main rotor. Then comes the radome covering the AW391 radar. Farther aft, the thick fuselage kinks upwards, with a six-bladed tail rotor to port and a horizontal stabiliser to starboard.

Weight empty: 6.08t   **Fuselage length:** 17m
Weight loaded: 9.53t   **Speed:** 112-144kt
Rotor span: 18.9m   **Range:** 664-814nm

Westland Wessex

The Westland Wessex was developed from the American Sikorsky S-58 which first flew in 1954. The British version entered FAA service in 1961.

The HAS Mk 3 has a single Gazelle gas-turbine, while the HU Mk 5 is powered by two Bristol Siddeley Gnome gas turbines coupled together.

Those Mk 3s still in service form 737 Squadron. They are equipped for anti-submarine warfare, carrying dunking sonar, with rocket pods outboard of the main undercarriage legs.

Above:
British Aerospace Sea Harrier.
Author's collection

Below:
A Westland Sea King helicopter fitted with Searchwater radar for airborne early warning. *Westland Helicopters*

Bottom:
The Royal Navy's first Westland Lynx helicopter operating from the Type 21 frigate HMS *Amazon* in May 1977.

The Mk 5 can also be used as an anti-submarine helicopter or for Commando assault (lifting 16 fully equipped troops). It is in service with 707 and 771 Squadrons (aircrew training at Yeovilton and Culdrose). Those with 772 at Portland are employed as required by the ships exercising off that base. There are also 847 and 858 Squadrons (both anti-submarine). The Navy currently has 150 Wessex on its strength.

From the side, the Wessex fuselage has the appearance of a 'horse-faced' narrow triangle. Its wheeled undercarriage is fixed. The bulbous nose houses the powerplant. The pilots are seated high up in a streamlined fairing which also supports the four-bladed main rotor. If search radar is carried, its dorsal radome is located here. The tail extension carried a four-bladed rotor and a small horizontal stabiliser.

Weight, empty: 3.93t
Weight loaded: 6.12t
Rotor span: 17.07m

Fuselage length: 14.74m
Speed: 100-110kt
Range: 410nm

Westland Lynx HAS Mk 2

A joint Westland-Aerospatiale venture, the Lynx first flew in 1971. Although capable of the usual helicopter liaison and air-sea rescue duties, the Lynx is very much a strike aircraft, designed as an integral part of warship armament against surface and submarine targets. It can 'dunk' its own sonar, or be directed into an attack position by its parent warship. From there, the helicopter can drop two Mk 11 depth-charges or launch two homing torpedoes, either the Mk 46 or the latest Stingray. Against fast attack craft or larger surface warships, the missile employed is the Sea Skua, a low-level radar-guided weapon. These stores are carried on pylons on each side of the fuselage.

The Lynx is currently in service with 702 and 815 Squadrons. Virtually all are posted to destroyers and frigates, but some of 702 Squadron are stationed at Yeovilton for aircrew training.

The Lynx has a fixed wheeled undercarriage. Its pointed nose (containing Seaspray radar for Sea Skua guidance) projects from beneath the two pilots' feet.

Dorsal streamlining covers the two Rolls-Royce Gem gas turbines, and supports the four-bladed main rotor. The fuselage kinks upwards to carry a four-bladed tail rotor to port and a horizontal stabiliser to starboard.

A total of 88 Lynx are in service.

Weight empty: 2.66t
Weight loaded: 4.76t
Rotor span: 12.8m

Fuselage length: 11.92m (to tail rotor centre)
Speed: 70-180kt
Range: 340nm

Westland Wasp HAS Mk 1

The original design first flew in 1958, the Royal Navy's first Wasp taking off in 1962.

Most of the 80 in service are allocated to 829 Squadron which provides anti-submarine helicopters for frigates. In this role, the Wasp carries one Mk 46 homing torpedo on each side of the fuselage. Three passengers can be transported, so the Wasp makes a useful liaison aircraft, and is therefore issued by 829 Squadron to survey ships. It also means that Wasps can be seen at many establishments such as Portland (aircrew training with 703 Squadron).

The Wasp has a four-wheeled fixed undercarriage. The cockpit canopy appears rather angular above a somewhat bulbous nose. The Bristol Siddeley Nimbus gas-turbine is completely exposed beneath the lattice pylon for the four-bladed main rotor. Right aft, the fuselage kinks upwards to support the two-bladed tail rotor.

Weight empty: 1.47t	**Fuselage length:** 10m
Weight loaded: 2.5t	**Speed:** 95-112kt
Rotor Span: 9.8m	**Range:** 235nm

Westland Gazelle HT Mk 2

Developed jointly by Westlands of Yeovil and Aerospatiale of France, the prototype Gazelle first flew in 1967. The first of the Royal Navy's Gazelles Mk 2, entered service in 1974. The principal role of the 18 on the strength of the Fleet Air Arm, is as a pilot trainer with 705 Squadron at Culdrose. Royal Marine pilots also fly the Gazelle for liaison and reconnaissance.

The Gazelle has a skid undercarriage. The trainee and instructor-pilots sit in an almost fully-glazed, backward-curving nose compartment. The Turbomeca Astazou gas-turbine is visibly mounted on top of the fuselage, directly beneath the three-bladed main rotor. The tail rotor is located within a fin and tailplane assembly reminiscent of a fixed-wing aircraft.

Weight empty: 0.91t	**Fuselage length:** 9.53m
Weight loaded: 1.8t	**Speed:** 126-167kt
Rotor span: 10.5m	**Range:** 193.5-361nm

Fixed-Wing Aircraft

English Electric Canberra T4, TT18 and T22

The Canberra first flew in 1949. Designed as an RAF bomber, it was subsequently adapted in photo-reconnaissance, night-intruder and training versions. A number are still used by various research and other aeronautical bodies. The seven based at Yeovilton belong to the Navy's Fleet Requirements & Direction Unit. They serve as targets for radar and gunnery calibration, carry out photographic work, and guide pilotless radio-controlled drones which are expendable and can be shot down with live missiles. They also provide experience for aircraft direction officers during training. Most FAA machines are painted a dark navy blue, but the FRADU Canberras are a light bluish-grey, with yellow markings.

The Canberra has a cylindrical streamlined fuselage, with glazed nose and separate cockpit canopy for the crew of three. Set halfway back, are the broad-chord, low-aspect ratio wings. The two Rolls-Royce Avon jet engines are buried in wing-mounted cylindrical nacelles. The single fin and rudder and tailplane are of angular appearance.

Weight empty: 12.63t	**Length:** 19.96m
Weight loaded: 24.92t	**Speed:** 440-500kt
Wing Span: 19.51m	**Range:** 700-2,600nm

Hawker Hunter GA11, T8C and T8M

A single-seat interceptor fighter which first flew in 1951, the Hunter was subsequently adapted for photo-reconnaissance, ground attack and as a dual-control trainer. Although never navalised for carrier-borne operations, eight Hunters have been allocated to the FAA for employment with FRADU at Yeovilton. They are painted a dark bluey-green above, and very light duck-egg blue or white below.

The Hunter has a pointed nose. The air intakes for the single Rolls-Royce Avon jet engine are located at the wing roots, exhausting through the tail. The wings (mid-way up the fuselage and appearing more rounded than the Sea Harrier's), the tail-fin and tailplane are all swept back. It has a tricycle undercarriage, retracting into the nose and wings.

Weight empty: 5.90t   **Length:** 13.98m
Weight loaded: 10.89t   **Speed:** 450-560kt
Wing span: 10.25m   **Range:** 1,630nm

British Aerospace Sea Harrier FRS Mk 1

Popularly known as a 'jump-jet', the Sea Harrier is technically designated a vertical short take-off and landing (V/STOL) aircraft.

The prototype RAF Harrier flew in 1966, the navalised version being delivered in 1977.

It is a reconnaissance strike fighter, carrying out attacks against surface targets on land and sea, yet able to engage enemy aircraft in combat. It thus augments the aerial defences of the fleet, and acts as a long-range bombardment weapon. At other times, its reconnaissance equipment enables the fleet commander to see beyond the horizon.

There are 30 Sea Harriers in service with 800, 801 (*Invincible*), 809 (*Illustrious*) and 899 (Yeovilton) squadrons.

The slim nose contains Blue Fox radar. Below its dielectric covering, is the panel through which the camera takes its photographs. The pilot's canopy is angled forward, giving him a good view when landing on.

The cockpit equipment includes a voice recorder, so that he can describe what he sees during reconnaissance missions. The cockpit is flanked by two huge 'elephant-ear' intakes for the single Rolls-Royce-Bristol Pegasus jet engine. A flight refuelling probe is located above the port intake. The jet thrust of the engine is directed through rotating nozzles and vanes in the fuselage, two on each side beneath the shoulder-mounted wings. There are also four very small nozzles (known as 'puffers') in the nose, the tail, and at the wing tips. These maintain balance during hovering and in the transition between vertical and horizontal flight — and even when flying backwards. These devices not only enable the Sea Harrier to operate from very restricted spaces, but also make it extremely manoeuvrable in air-to-air combat. The wings, tail-fin and tailplane are all swept back, with rather pointed tips giving the aircraft something of an 'anchor' appearance. The Harrier must be the only supersonic (in a dive) fighter without a fully retractable undercarriage. The main wheels disappear into the fuselage, but the stabiliser wheels are still just visible when their outrigger legs are retracted into the wingtips. A variety of war stores can be carried beneath the wings and the fuselage. To the latter is usually fixed a pair of single 30mm gun pods. Between them can be attached a 450kg bomb or a pod containing five cameras.

Meanwhile the four wing mountings can hold combinations of 450kg bombs, Sidewinder heatseeking or Sky Flash radar-homing air-to-air missiles, and Sea Eagle active-radar-guided seaskimming anti-ship missiles with an estimated range of 60nm. There is also a two-seat training version, the T4N.

Weight empty: 5.53t
Weight loaded: 11.34t
Wing span: 7.7m
Length: 14.5m
Speed: 640kt
Range: 250-400nm

De Havilland Sea Heron C1/C4

An enlarged development of the de Havilland Dove, the Heron light transport first flew in 1950. Four are employed as liaison aircraft in the Fleet Air Arm, retaining the appearance of a civilian airliner. Seventeen passengers can be carried.

The Heron has a pointed nose with a curvy tail fin, but its tailplane and low wings are rather angular. It has four de Havilland Gipsy Queen inline piston engines, each driving a two-bladed propeller.

Weight empty: 3.69t
Weight loaded: 6.13t
Wing span: 21.8m
Length: 14.78m
Speed: 160kt
Range: 800nm

Scottish Aviation Jetstream T Mks 2 and 3

The original Jetstream light transport was built by Handley Page and first flew in 1967. It was subsequently produced by Scottish Aviation of Prestwick and in 1973 proved adaptable as a training aircraft. Some are thus employed by the RAF, while the 16 in the FAA are stationed at Culdrose in 750 (Observer Training) Squadron.

The work of a Royal Navy observer entails much more than just looking out of the window. He has to operate navigational equipment, radar, sonar, and electronic countermeasures. He has to process and evaluate the information thus acquired, identify targets, arm, and then fire a variety of weapons. In addition, he *is* looking out of the window; using his own eyes, assessing what he sees, recording it on tape, film, notepaper or in memory, then reporting intelligently, either by radio or in later personal debriefing. He must be able to do all this in every condition of weather and regardless of what the aircraft is doing. And as well as all this, he has to watch out for hostile aircraft, missiles or gunfire — in short, he does everything except fly the aircraft. All these skills (except the actual firing of live weapons) can be learned in the Jetstream.

The Jetstream looks like a civilian airliner with a row of cabin windows. It has an elongated nose and a swept-back tail fin, but the high tailplane and the low wings are not swept back. The two three-bladed Turbomeca Astazou turboprop engine nacelles project well forward of the wings. The tricycle undercarriage is fully retractable. New aircraft will be equipped with belly-mounted radar.

Weight empty: 3.49t
Weight loaded: 5.70t
Wing span: 15.85m
Length: 14.37m
Speed: 234-300kt
Range: 1,200nm

The Organisation of the Royal Navy

Its Administration

Until 1964, the Royal Navy was administered by the Board of Admiralty, its senior serving officer was the First Sea Lord, and its political head was the First Lord of the Admiralty with a seat in the Cabinet. Even after the formation of the unified Ministry of Defence, the three Services still maintained a large degree of independence, each of the three Service chiefs advising the Minister of Defence regarding their respective Service.

The recently announced re-organisation of the MoD which is still being implemented, is intended to result in a greater unity in practice as well as in theory. What follows is a general outline of the new organisation, and it should be remembered that Civil Servants are represented at every level along with Service representatives.

The organisation is headed by the Secretary of State for Defence (usually known as the Minister of Defence) with a seat in the Cabinet.

The Minister's senior military adviser is the Chief of the Defence Staff. A serving soldier, sailor or airman, he — or she — will be the sole spokesperson for all the Services.

The CDS is advised by — and gives orders to — the Defence Staff. This is presided over by the Vice-Chief of the Defence Staff (again, a soldier, sailor or airman). The Defence Staff consists of three Deputy Chiefs of the Defence Staff. The three DCDS may be all soldiers or all sailors or all airmen, or two from one Service and one from another, or one from each Service — the combination and original Service is immaterial. One DCDS is responsible for the operations of all three Services, one for the equipment of all three Services, and one for the personnel and priorities of all three Services.

Subordinate to the Defence Staff are 11 senior posts. Three of these are held by senior officers of the Army, Royal Navy and Royal Air Force. It seems that these Service chiefs will be virtually managers, carrying out the orders of the Defence Staff, but obviously the Defence Staff will have to listen to the advice of the Service chiefs.

Whether the individual traditions of the three Services will mean that they inevitably diverge and eventually become virtually independent (though fully co-operational) once more, or whether future soldiers, sailors and airmen will envisage themselves as members of a single defence team rather than members of a separate Army, Navy or Air Force, remains to be seen. What is hoped will be most likely, is that the three Services will appear completely separate to the outsider, while their maintenance and direction stemming from unified policy results in unified strategy — the three services being wielded as a single, but multi-bladed, weapon.

Its Ships

The sea-going operational ships of the Royal Navy form the Fleet.

C-in-C Fleet flies his flag in HMS *Warrior*, a shore establishment at Eastbury Park, Northwood, Middlesex. (He is thus able to issue orders to the Fleet at any time and in any situation. If he were in a warship at sea during some crisis, he would be subject to the usual restrictions regarding transmissions which can give away positions; he might not be able to transmit at all.)

C-in-C Fleet is also NATO Allied C-in-C Channel and C-in-C Eastern Atlantic Area. Flag Officer Submarines shares *Warrior* with the C-in-C and is also NATO COMSUBEASTLANT.

The Fleet is divided into First Flotilla, Second Flotilla, Third Flotilla, Submarine Command, and Mine Counter-Measures Command. These are further subdivided as follows:

FIRST FLOTILLA
One 'County' class light cruiser/destroyer as flagship plus
   1st Frigate Squadron (7 frigates)
   3rd Destroyer Squadron (4 destroyers)
   6th Frigate Squadron (6 frigates)
   7th Frigate Squadron (8 frigates)

SECOND FLOTILLA
Two 'County' class light cruisers/destroyers and one 'Battleaxe' class frigate as flag squadron plus:
   2nd Frigate Squadron (5 frigates)
   4th Frigate Squadron (5 frigates)
   5th Destroyer Squadron (5 destroyers)
   8th Frigate Squadron (7 frigates)

THIRD FLOTILLA

Ark Royal	Fearless
Invincible	Intrepid
Illustrious	Endurance
Bristol	

SUBMARINE COMMAND
1st Squadron (Gosport — 7 patrol submarines)
2nd Squadron (Devonport — 5 fleet submarines)
3rd Squadron (Faslane — 4 fleet and 2 patrol submarines)
10th Squadron (Faslane — 3 Polaris submarines)

MINE COUNTER-MEASURES COMMAND
1st Squadron (Rosyth)
2nd Squadron (Portsmouth)
Fishery Protection Squadron (Rosyth)
10th Squadron (RNR)

Above left:
The badge of the Polaris submarine HMS *Revenge*.

Above:
The badge of the Type 22 frigate HMS *Broadsword*.

Left:
The radar-directed Vulcan/Phalanx anti-aircraft and anti-missile gun as mounted in the aircraft carriers *Invincible*, *Illustrious* and *Ark Royal*.

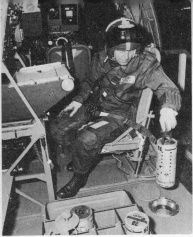

Left:
A Sea King crewman shows how a sonobuoy is deployed from a helicopter.

Below:
Three LCUs and an LCVP from HMS *Intrepid* disembarking Royal Marines and their equipment. Note the 'bobbin' unrolling a flexible roadway over the beach.

Bottom left:
A surgeon-lieutenant in the WRNS.

Bottom right:
Many RNR personnel serve in MCMVs as part of their training and seagoing experience.

It should be noted that these numbers of ships are those allocated to those squadrons. It does not mean that they are all in company all the time; some will be away refitting or on a detached service. Indeed, whole squadrons may be temporarily transferred from their parent flotilla to accompany, say, the Third Flotilla, on some special operation. It should also be noted that each frigate squadron is composed of vessels drawn from a variety of classes over the whole age-range of the fleet. Each group is thus a self-contained balanced task force without any one squadron consisting entirely of older ships. This means that the ageing warships have to be maintained to the latest standards, and have to be discarded and replaced as soon as it becomes too difficult to incorporate the newest equipment during regular refit.

Royal Marines

Serving on land and sea, they provide the Commando units for amphibious assault, specialist personnel manning landing craft, flying helicopters and firing guns and missiles, as well as fighting as infantrymen. Some operate the Special Boat Service for clandestine raids on enemy coasts. More officers and other ranks are involved in intelligence work ashore and technical duties afloat. And no traditional ceremony of the Royal Navy seems complete without the presence of a Royal Marine Band.

Women's Royal Naval Service
Officers and ratings perform technical and administrative duties at all levels throughout the Navy.

Women's Royal Marines
Perform similar duties as the WRNS, but as part of the Royal Marines.

Queen Alexandra's Royal Naval Nursing Service
Provide nursing staff in RN hospitals ashore and sick quarters ashore, and in hospital ships afloat. Their ranks of Nursing Officer, Senior Nursing Officer, Superintending Nursing Officer, Chief Nursing Officer, Principal Nursing Officer, and Director of Nursing Services (formerly Matron-in-Chief), correspond to those from Lieutenant to Commodore RN. Naval Nurse, Senior Naval Nurse, Assistant Head Naval Nurse and Head Naval Nurse are rating equivalents of Able Seaman to Chief Petty Officer.

Royal Naval Reserve
Although some instructors are attached permanently to the Royal Naval Reserve and the Women's Royal Naval Reserve, the Reserve is mainly a body of part-time personnel who meet for training one or two nights a week and at weekends. For a longer period once a year, they have practical seagoing experience in one of the coastal minesweepers allocated to the Reserve. The personnel undertaking these training courses (both men and women) are of three persuasions; officers and ratings who have retired from the regular Navy, but are still on the Active Reserve List; people in full-time civilian employment who wish to perform some service in the Navy; young officers at university, whose undergraduate studies are being paid for by the Navy as a condition of their service.

The RNR is organised in divisions, each one having a title as well as being commissioned as an RN shore establishment. Each one also has a seagoing vessel attached to it, but these can vary according to the Navy's operational requirements.

Title	Location	HM Ship	Sea-going Training Ship
London	King's Reach	*President*	*Humber*
Clyde	Glasgow	*Graham*	*Attacker* and
	Greenock	*Dalriada*	*Dovey*
Falmouth	(being formed)		
Forth	Edinburgh	*Claverhouse*	*Spey*
Hull	(being formed)		
Mersey	Princes Dock, Liverpool	*Eaglet*	*Ribble*
	Liverpool University		*Striker*
Severn	Bristol	*Flying Fox*	*Carron*
Solent	Eastern Docks, Southampton	*Wessex*	*Itchen*
	Southampton University		*Fencer*
South Wales	East Dock, Cardiff	*Cambria*	*Waveney*
Sussex	Hove	*Sussex*	*Arun*
Tay	Dundee	*Camperdown*	*Helmsdale* and *Abinger*
	Aberdeen University		*Chaser*
Tyne	Gateshead	*Calliope*	*Orwell*
Ulster	Belfast	*Caroline*	*Helford*
Gibraltar	The Dockyard	*Calpe*	

The insignia of the RNR is the same as that of the RN, but with the addition of the letter 'R' within the curl of the cuff.

Royal Marines Reserve and Women's Royal Marine Reserve
People of similar persuasions as those in the RNR, who undergo training in similar fashion, but with the Royal Marines. They are organised in the following divisions:

RMR City of London
RMR Scotland
RMR Bristol
RMR Merseyside
RMR Tyne

Royal Fleet Auxiliary Service
Although the Navy owns its tankers, storeships, logistic transports and other ocean-going support vessels, it has been customary for them to be of merchant ship appearance and for them to be registered as merchant ships.

This has enabled them to enter the ports of other nations to load cargo, without first seeking the formal diplomatic permission which has to be obtained for visiting warships. And at the end of their service career, these ships may still have several years of useful life in them, so they can be sold to a commercial company.

Their mercantile status has also meant that their crews are civilians and not subject to the Naval Discipline Act. This does not imply any slackness aboard RFAs, but that all matters regarding rates of pay, pension rights, overtime payment, leave, qualifications for promotion, and the wearing of uniform, are agreed between private management (usually a commercial shipping company) and the National Union of Seamen or other professional body. The Admiralty Board is thus relieved of much of that debate, although stipulating that the conditions of service or charter expect vessel and personnel to be where the MoD requires them to be, and doing what the Navy wants — and that may include acting as convoy so that warships can exercise escort procedures.

Like all other merchantmen, RFAs are entitled to be armed in wartime for their own self-defence. All RFAs are equipped for the speedy installation of weapons, and some carry guns of 20-40mm calibre all the time, but in a boxed condition. However, several have had to be armed more openly when serving in areas of undeclared hostility. Indeed, most large RFAs now embark anti-submarine helicopters, not only for vertical replenishment, but also for additional protection when fuelling or storing the fleet at sea. Because of this, and because of the quantity and sometimes controversial nature of war-stores now being carried, some nations have declared that RFAs are warships, not merchantmen.

Furthermore, the very act of transferring fuel and ammunition at sea, and the conditions under which this has to be practised, sometimes conflict with the British Board of Trade regulations regarding the carriage and handling of dangerous cargoes. Accordingly it has been decided to deregister these vessels as merchant ships. Presumably, prior permission will now have to be sought before they can enter a foreign port. However, their crews will still be considered as merchant seamen. Nor will existing safety standards be relaxed.

RFAs wear the Blue Ensign of the Royal Naval Reserve with a gold vertical anchor in the fly.

Royal Maritime Auxiliary Service (RMAS)

Operates sea-going boom defence vessels, tugs and salvage craft. Being civilian vessels, they wear the Red Ensign, unless their Master is a member of the RNR, in which case the Blue Ensign is worn. The same applies to the vessels of what was the Port Auxiliary Service (PAS) which is now incorporated in the RMAS. The PAS performed a similar service as the RMAS, but in smaller craft, and in and around dockyards.

It has always been the custom for dockyard craftsmen and artisans to be civilians, but nowadays many 'housekeeping' tasks in RN shore establishments are also performed by civilians. These include the operation of fleet tenders, driving and maintaining motor-transport, and general cleaning of offices and internal roadways. In previous generations, this work was done by sailors who had to be accommodated somewhere, creating further 'household' and movement problems within the complex. They had to go through joining procedures, apply for leave and be found jobs to do when not actually cleaning buildings or driving boats or buses. All this required more administrative, catering and regulating personnel to organise, feed and police a swelling number of ratings who seemed never to go to sea and in due course of time, did not seem to *want* to go to sea. And if there were not enough of them, then defaulters or men passing through the barracks were assigned such duties — and because it was done unwillingly, it had to be supervised and inspected by yet another group of ratings and officers. With such numbers of people involved, barracks became too crowded, so obsolescent warships often found employment as spare accommodation vessels. They might not be expected to go to sea again, but all their internal machinery had to be maintained for habitable conditions, and they had to be regularly docked. But nowadays, by employing civilians or by putting out to civilian contract as many non-warlike, shorebased jobs as possible, the Navy has been spared a whole range of maintenance, administrative and discipline problems, while keeping as many warships at sea as much as possible.

A common phrase used by outsiders when critically discussing the subject, is 'The Navy — what there is of it!', comparing it unfavourably with bygone fleets. Certainly roadsteads may have appeared full of warships in previous periods, but not all of them were fit for sea. Even those that were — the great battleships, especially — took so long to raise steam, that it was simpler for them to spend weeks at a time swinging round a buoy performing harbour evolutions. And those which did depart for foreign stations were very often employed as ocean-going barracks, moving large numbers of men from place to place, so that seawise personnel could be despatched ashore on tasks which today are performed by the Army or by local civil defence, or even by a charitable relief organisation. The Royal Navy today is indeed smaller in numbers of men and ships, but the majority of both are fit for sea, and most of them are at sea, or at any rate proceed to sea for daily operations or exercises. Whether there are enough to cope with several simultaneous emergencies, is another matter — but then, in such situations, there never are enough.

Royal Naval Auxiliary Service (RNXS)
Provides training for part-time personnel prepared to serve in the Royal Fleet Auxiliary or the Royal Maritime Auxiliary Service. The relationship of the RNXS to these organisations is similar to the relationship between the RNR and the RN.

Naval Recruiting Department
There are recruiting offices in most cities and major towns, often far from the sea. The country is divided into the following regions:

London	Scottish
West Midland	South-West
East Midland	Southern
North-West	

Sea Cadet Corps
In existence in 1856 and officially established from 1899 onwards, the Sea Cadet Corps provides disciplined and adventurous activity for boys and girls between the ages of 12 and 18. There is no compulsion for members to join

the Navy later, but obviously Sea Cadets get some idea of what life is like in the Service.

The Sea Cadet Corps is recognised as a Voluntary Youth Organisation by the Department of Education and Science, and by other relevant education authorities. At the same time the MoD is responsible for the supervision of training, RN officers being appointed in charge of each Sea Cadet area.

Cadet ranks according to age and ability, are as follows (there are equivalent ranks for the Marine Cadet Section and the Girls' Nautical Training Contingent, both of which are integral components of the Corps):

Cadet Petty Officer	Cadet Able Seaman
Cadet Leading Seaman	Cadet Ordinary Seaman
Age 15	Junior Cadet.

Above the age of 18, cadets can remain in the Corps as voluntary Instructors, becoming Petty Officer Instructors above the age of 20. Voluntary officers of the Sea Cadet Corps who are not serving members of the Royal Navy wear 'wavy' rings on their cuffs.

Sea Cadet Corps Headquarters is at Broadway House, Broadway, Wimbledon, London SW19 1RL (Tel 01-540 8222). There are six areas, each with its own office as follows:

Northern: (Northern Ireland, Scotland and Northeast England); Sea Cadet Corps, 1 Forbes Road, Rosyth KY11 2AN (Tel Inverkeithing 0383-416300).

Eastern: (England east of the Pennines, Northeast Midlands and East Anglia): SCC, RAF Swinderby, Lincoln LN6 9QE (Tel Swinderby 052-286 477).

North-West: (Northern half of Wales, England west of the Pennines, Northwest Midlands): SCC, HMS *Eaglet*, Princes Dock Liverpool L3 0AA (Tel 051-236 7377).

South-West: (Southern half of Wales, Southwest Midlands, Southwest Peninsula): SCC, Room 11, Block C, MoD, Ensleigh, Bath, Avon BA1 5AD (Tel 0225-67550/67729).

Southern: (Southeast Midlands, England south of the Thames): SCC, HMS *Nelson*, Portsmouth PO1 3HH (Tel 0705-822351, ext 24263).

London: (Greater London and Essex): SCC, Room 2601, Empress State Building, Lillie Road, Fulham SW6 1TR (Tel 01-385 1244, ext 3166).

Each area is divided into districts, each of the latter comprising three to 12 SCC units. There are some 400 units altogether, each one having its own number and name prefixed by 'Training Ship', eg TS *Swiftsure*. Each unit has its own Unit Committee of local people who supervise the general running of the unit, raise funds and promote the movement as a whole. In addition most units have a Parents' and Supporters' Association. Many units have their own band, and there is great emphasis on first aid, communications, seamanship and boatwork. There are opportunities for visits to RN ships and establishments, plus sail training in the brig *Royalist*. The obsolescent guided missile destroyer *Kent* has just been adapted as a harbour accommodation ship for Sea Cadets attending courses in the Portsmouth area.

Boys and girls wishing to join the Sea Cadet Corps, its Royal Marine Section, or the Girls' Nautical Training Contingent, can obtain further information either from SCC Headquarters, or from the appropriate area office, or from their nearest unit; its address will be in the telephone directory under 'Sea Cadet Corps'.

Volunteer Cadet Corps
Attached to Naval and Marine shore establishments, their age limits are from nine to 15 years. Each unit is raised and controlled by a local committee composed of officers and men of the various establishments.

Royal Naval Volunteer Cadet Corps
Portsmouth area: *Victory*; *Excellent*; *Vernon*; *Dolphin*; *Dryad*; *Collingwood*. Devonport area: *Drake*.

Royal Marine Volunteer Cadet Corps
Portsmouth Company (Royal Marine Barracks, Eastney); Plymouth Company (Royal Marine Barracks, Stonehouse); Deal Company (Royal Marine Depot, Deal).

Total of Personnel
RN & RM Officers	9,800
RN & RM Ratings and Other Ranks	58,400
Servicewomen	3,500
Regular Reserve (1982)	25,800
Regular Reserve, Women (1982)	100
RNR (1982)	4,300
RNR Women (1982)	1,100
RMR Regular	2,100
RMR Volunteers	1,000
RNR Air Branch Officers	80
	106,180

The Royal Navy and NATO

The Royal Navy exercises regularly with the forces of the other member states of the North Atlantic Treaty Organisation, for in time of war involving all these countries, they would all come under NATO command. Until then, ships, aircraft and armies remain under their own national command, and can be employed in campaigns of limited objective. British ships and personnel may also be stationed in areas under the command of other NATO nationals.

The Historic Royal Navy

Note: Admission charges, opening hours and opening days may vary, especially according to season. Closing time is sometimes the time of last admission and sometimes the time when all visitors must be off the premises. It can be assumed that all museums are closed on Christmas Day, while many are closed on other Bank Holidays as well. Admission charges may include all facilities or only some, additional charges being made for special or temporary exhibitions or other events.

National Maritime Museum

Romney Road, Greenwich, London SE10 9NF. Tel (01)-858 4422.

The National Maritime Museum employs models, relics, uniforms, literature, paintings, technical archives, ephemera, full-sized dioramas and audio-visual presentations to portray the whole of Britain's experience of the sea, from prehistoric times to the present day. Complete craft up to tug-size can be accommodated in the largest gallery, with even bigger exhibits being located at the Museum's out-stations in the southwest of England. The nearby *Cutty Sark* and *Gipsy Moth IV* are not part of the National Maritime Museum's collections, but no reference to the maritime associations of Greenwich is complete without their mention.

Although the National Maritime Museum is not devoted solely to the history of the Royal Navy, that Service has obviously played a significant role in Britain's maritime history — a role reflected in the Museum's displays. There are not only relics and paintings of naval heroes and battles (such as the uniform Nelson wore at Trafalgar), but there is also emphasis on the Royal Navy's contribution to peaceful maritime development, such as exploration and navigation. There are thus close links with the Old Royal Observatory at the top of the hill behind the Museum, of which it is a part. Located on the Greenwich Meridian, the Observatory has its own exhibitions and a planetarium, and also explains the history of the search for accurate time on which the calculation of longitude depends.

Open: Mondays-Saturdays 10.00-18.00 (17.00 in winter); Sundays: 14.00-17.30 (17.00 in winter).
Closed: New Year's Day; Good Friday; Christmas Eve; Christmas Day; Boxing Day.
Admission (to National Maritime Museum & Old Royal Observatory): £1.50 Adults (£1 to a single site, ie Main Building or Observatory), 75p Children,

Students, Disabled, Unemployed and OAPs (50p to single site), £4 Family Ticket (two adults and up to five children); 40p Local Residents (20p for half-price categories).
Facilities for disabled: Lower Ground Floor only — East and West Wings.
Nearest Stations: Maze Hill; Greenwich. (Also boat trips from Westminster and Charing Cross.)

Scottish United Services Museum

The Castle, Edinburgh. Tel (031)-226 6907.

The Naval Gallery of the Scottish United Services Museum is at present located in the Palace Block on the east side of Crown Square adjacent to the Scottish National War Memorial in Edinburgh Castle, situated on a rocky cliff high above Edinburgh. There are ship models, relics and paintings of naval battles and heroes. These date from the Old Scots Navy of Stewart times (with reference to Admiral Sir Andrew Barton), through the age of fighting sail with Duncan and Cochrane, to modern admirals of Scottish descent, such as Cunningham. In addition, many famous warships were constructed in Scottish yards, but Scotland's contribution to maritime history is not confined to the Royal Navy. Captain John Paul (Jones), Father of the American Navy, was a Scotsman and he too is commemorated here — a reminder of the close links between the RN and the USN which are reflected in almost every display of naval history in the country.

Open: Mondays-Saturdays 09.30-18.00 (17.15 November-April); Sundays 11.00-18.00 (12.30-16.30 November-April).
Closed: New Year's Day; 2 January; Christmas Day; Boxing Day; some Sundays during Military Tattoos and their preparation.
Admission: £1.70 Adults (reduction for Children and OAPs). Although entry to the Museum itself is free, its opening times are inseparably linked with the Castle, for which there is an admission charge; it is these details which are quoted here.
Nearest station: Edinburgh

Sussex Combined Forces Museum

Redoubt Fortress, Royal Parade, Eastbourne. Tel (0323)-33952.

Just as the National Maritime Musem and the Scottish United Services Museum show how the Royal Navy fits into national history, so many thematic museums (such as the Science Museum in South Kensington, London) have exhibits illustrating the RN's contribution to or influence on their particular areas of study. Regional museums too have galleries devoted to local maritime history, naval heroes, engagements and shipbuilding. This is particularly so in the Eastbourne Redoubt, which is a circular fortress built of brick in the Napoleonic period. It now houses exhibits illustrating the history of all three services in Sussex, including relics of the fleet minesweeper HMS *Eastbourne* and the cruiser HMS *Sussex* (both saw service in World War 2). The Redoubt itself, together with its associated Martello Tower, represents the combined Army-Navy weapons system designed to repulse Napoleon's threatened invasion.

Open: Daily Easter to November 10.00-17.00; other times by arrangement.
Admission: 30p Adults; 15p Children and OAPs (entry to Parade Ground and Gun Deck free).
Facilities for disabled: The Ground Floor, which contains all the actual exhibits, is fully accessible.
Nearest station: Eastbourne

The Mary Rose

HM Naval Base, Portsmouth, Hampshire. Tel (0705)-750521 or Tel (0705)-839766 for Press & Publicity Office, Old Bond Store, Portsmouth PO1 2ET.

Probably clinker-built (with overlapping planks of wood), soon after Henry VIII's accession in 1509, the *Mary Rose* was reconstructed in 1536. New carvel-planking (resulting in flush-fitting planks of wood) assisted the cutting of ports in her hull to carry the latest heavy guns with anti-ship (instead of anti-personnel) potential. On 19 July 1545 *Mary Rose* foundered in Spithead, while repelling a French task force attempting to enter Portsmouth Harbour, destroy the dockyard and land assault troops.

After two salvage attempts over the centuries, the *Mary Rose* was forgotten until relocated by Alexander McKee in 1967. There followed one of the world's great feats of marine archaeology. The climax came in 1982, when the *Mary Rose* was raised in a cradle and moved into Portsmouth Dockyard.

Much more of her timbers remain than one expects to see, wrapped in a dream-like mist from conservation sprays in the cathedral-sized Ship Hall. The *Mary Rose* still lies at the angle she rested on the seabed. Eventually she will be set upright, the sprays switched off, and much of her interior timbers replaced, so that visitors will be able to look into the sectioned hull, virtually complete except for her port side. Many of the small artefacts and an explanatory display are located in an Exhibition Hall just inside the Dockyard Main (or Victory) Gate. The *Mary Rose* Ship Hall itself is situated just beyond the stern of HMS *Victory*.

Open: Mondays-Saturdays 10.30-17.00 (March-October); 10.30-16.30 (November-February); Sundays 13.00-17.00 (March-October); 13.00-16.30 (November-February).
Closed: Christmas Day.
Admission to Ship Hall: £1 Adults; 50p Children, Students and OAPs; £2.50 Family Ticket (two adults and two children).
Admission to Exhibition Hall: £1.50 Adults; £1 Children, Students and OAPs; £4 Family Ticket (two adults and two children).
Nearest station: Portsmouth Harbour.

Buckland Abbey

Buckland Monachorum, Yelverton, Devon PL20 6EY (turn west off A386 at Yelverton). Tel (0822) 853607.

In 1278 a Cistercian monastery was founded in the valley of the River Tavy, south of Tavistock (where Francis Drake was later born, about 1540). Buckland Abbey was dissolved in 1539 and in 1541 was bought by Sir

Richard Grenville. His grandson (another Sir Richard Grenville) converted the property into a manor house in 1576. In 1581 Buckland Abbey was purchased by Sir Francis Drake, now a wealthy man after his circumnavigation of the globe. Buckland Abbey remained Drake's home during the years of the Armada and all the other operations against Spain. Sir Francis Drake died of dysentery off the Isthmus of Panama and was buried at sea in Nombre de Dios Bay. He outlived Sir Richard Grenville by five years, the latter a casualty of the last fight of the *Revenge* on 31 August 1591.

Owned by the National Trust and managed by Plymouth Corporation, Buckland Abbey thus has associations with two naval heroes of Elizabethan times. This is reflected in the naval exhibits housed there, which include the legendary Drake's Drum, together with models of ships from the 16th to the 20th centuries and a collection of bone ship models made by French prisoners of war.

Open: *Good Friday-30 September:* Mondays-Saturdays 11.00-18.00; Sundays 14.00-18.00.
October-Good Friday: Wednesdays, Saturdays and Sundays 14.00-17.00.
Closed: Winter Mondays, Tuesdays, Thursdays and Fridays; Christmas Day; Boxing Day; New Year's Day.
Admission: £1.20 Adults; 60p Children.

Chatham Dockyard Museum

Chatham, Kent.

Naval storehouses were hired on Jillyngham Wharf in 1547 and a mastpond may have existed at Chatham from 1570 onwards. A drydock was established there in 1581 and the first ship launched in 1585. However, it was the reign of Charles I which saw the expansion of the complex into what was then the nation's principal naval base, accommodating vessels and equipment financed with the controversial Ship Money tax. The Medway was well situated for operations against the chief enemy of the day Holland. But in 1665 the Dutch themselves entered the river, destroying the dockyard and burning or capturing the ships at anchor there. The place was laid out afresh in 1685, reconstructed in the 1700s and further developed during the Industrial Revolution. The personnel accommodated in HMS *Pembroke* (the Royal Naval Barracks built in 1901 and closed in 1976) usually came from the London area. The oldest buildings now in existence are the storehouses nearest the river, the dockyard church, the hemp store, the spinning room, the tarring house and the Admiral's (or Medway) House. A museum is being prepared in one of these old buildings, illustrating the maritime history of the Medway in general and of Chatham Dockyard in particular.

Nearest station: Chatham

Admiral Blake Museum

Blake Street, Bridgwater, Somerset. Tel (0278) 56127.

Although this museum has a variety of exhibits illustrating Monmouth's Rebellion and the local history of Sedgemoor, it is also the house where

Robert Blake was born in 1599. A scholar and merchant, he served in the Parliamentarian army during the English Civil War. He was renowned for his defence of Lyme and Taunton, but it was not until 1649 that he was appointed an admiral and general-at-sea. This seems to have been Blake's first association with the Navy, but he undertook his new task as though he had been studying seamanship and maritime warfare all his life. He fought battles, organised blockades and mounted amphibious operations against royalist privateers, the Dutch, Barbary corsairs, and Spain. Admiral Blake died of scorbutic fever as his flagship *George* was entering Plymouth Sound on 7 August 1657.

Although the fleet in which he served was not a 'Royal' Navy, he nevertheless established the professionalism of the RN. He was the first British admiral to *control* a fleet at sea, instead of merely presiding over a collection of warships. He also emphasised that it was the Navy's job to act as an instrument of government policy, whatever that government or policy, without itself getting embroiled in politics.

The museum contains a range of Blake memorabilia.

Open: Tuesdays-Saturdays 11.00-16.00.
Closed: Sundays, Mondays, Christmas Day, etc.
Admission: Free.
Nearest station: Bridgwater.

The Royal Marines Museum

Royal Marine Barracks, Eastney, Southsea, Hampshire PO4 9PX. Tel (0705) 22351 ext 6135.

Housed in the old RMA Officers' Mess (built in 1868), this museum covers every aspect of the history of the Royal Marines from 1664 to the present day. Fully-captioned cases of uniforms, diagrams and relics are enlivened by dioramas of audio-visual displays of such events as the Battle of Trafalgar and the Zeebrugge Raid.

The history of bands is imaginatively described as is the story of Hannah Snell, a female marine from 1745 to 1750. There are links with the United States Marine Corps, and the history is brought up to date with a section on the Falklands War. The museum also possesses an outstanding medal collection which includes all the VCs awarded to the Corps.

Open: Mondays-Fridays 10.00-16.30; Saturdays/Sundays 10.00-12.30.
Closed: Christmas Day to mid-January.
Admission: Free.
Car park: Free.

Hatchlands

East Clandon, Guildford, Surrey GU4 7RT (off A246 Guildford-Leatherhead Road). Tel (0483) 222787.

The Honourable Edward Boscawen is a typical representative of the admirals of the 18th century. He was born in 1711, a Cornishman of such dash and pugnacity that he was nicknamed 'Old Dreadnought'. Admiral Boscawen proved fortunate in his commands and adventures, becoming

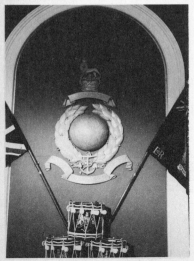

Top:
The Royal Naval College, Greenwich, seen from Island Gardens on the Isle of Dogs. The white building between the two Wren domes is the Queen's House, constructed by Inigo Jones for Queen Henrietta Maria and now part of the National Maritime Museum. On the hilltop behind can be glimpsed the statue of General Wolfe with the Old Royal Observatory to the right. *Author*

Above:
Resting on her starboard side at an angle of 60deg, the *Mary Rose* is seen here during a break in the systematic spraying of the woodwork to maintain 95% humidity. *Mary Rose Trust*

Left:
The badge of the Royal Marines in the Corps Museum at Eastney. *Author*

Right:
The figure of Captain Cook in his birthplace and Museum at Marton near Middlesbrough.
Capt Cook Museum

Below:
Buckler's Hard.
Buckler's Hard Museum

Bottom:
Nelson's Dockyard, Antigua.
Antigua & Barbuda Tourist Office

wealthy enough to purchase the estate of Hatchlands in Surrey. In 1758 he soon commissioned Robert Adam as interior decorator, but the Admiral did not spend much time in the building. An able administrator, in 1758 Boscawen commanded the amphibious force which captured Louisburg and Cape Breton Island, thus paving the way for Wolfe's conquest of Canada. In 1759 Boscawen's insistence on continual training and exercises regardless of conditions on blockade, enabled the Mediterranean Fleet to make a speedy departure from Gibraltar, overhauling a French squadron and defeating it off the Portuguese city of Lagos. Like many navalmen, his bluff exterior cloaked a romantic, almost poetic, streak in his character. Away from home at harvest-time, he wrote to his wife: 'To be sure I lose the fruits of the earth, but I am gathering the fruits of the sea'. Hatchlands was completed in 1759, but in 1760 Boscawen went to sea again, returning home to die on 10 January 1761. His life and naval career are described in the Boscawen Exhibition Room in this National Trust property.

Open: *April-14 October:* Wednesdays, Thursdays and Sundays 14.00-18.00.
Closed: Mondays, Tuesdays, Fridays, Saturdays and all winter.
Admission: £1 Adults; 50p Children.
Facilities for disabled: Garden and Ground Floor only.

Captain Cook's Birthplace and Museum

Stewart Park, Marton, Middlesbrough, Cleveland. Tel (0642) 311211.

The most famous representative of the Royal Navy's explorers, was born in Marton in 1728. A self-educated farmboy, he rose to command in the Merchant Navy; then started at the bottom again in the Royal Navy to become a peerless navigator, dietician, naturalist and leader of men.

This purpose-built museum describes the whole of Captain Cook's life and career, plus the places which he visited and discovered before his murder on Hawaii in 1779.

Open: Daily 10.00-18.00 (16.00 in winter).
Closed: Christmas Day; New Year's Day.
Admission: 30p Adults; 10p Children and OAPs.
Facilities for disabled: Specially designed for the disabled, with ramps and railings and disabled toilets (the museum has won an award for these facilities).
Nearest station: Marton. There is also a large car park in Stewart Park.

Buckler's Hard Maritime Museum

Beaulieu, Hampshire. Tel (059-063) 203.

Buckler's Hard was founded in the 1720s by the 2nd Duke of Montagu, who intended it to be a thriving port. The scheme failed, and by 1740 only two houses had been completed. However, the village then grew into an important shipyard. A large number of vessels including Nelson's *Agamemnon*, were launched there between 1745 and 1822. The shipyard was closed by the 1840s, but a century later Buckler's Hard became an important assembly point for the Normandy landings. The Maritime Museum, opened in 1963, comprises static exhibits of shipbuilding, navigation and life at sea.

There is a reconstruction of the New Inn as it was in 1795, together with a labourer's and a shipwright's cottage. At the Master Builder's House (now a hotel) Henry Adams's study has been reconstructed.

Open: *October-Easter daily:* 10.00-16.30; *Easter-Whitsun daily:* 10.00-18.00; *Whitsun-September daily:* 10.00-21.00.
Closed: Christmas Day.
Admission: £1.50 Adults; 50p Children and OAPs.
Facilities for disabled: Ground Floor of museum.

HMS Victory

HM Naval Base, Portsmouth, Hampshire. Tel (0705)-822351 extn 22571.

Dominating the skyline over Portsmouth Dockyard are the three masts of HMS *Victory*. She was laid down at Chatham in 1759, launched in 1765 and commissioned in 1778. Her hull is 69m long, and carries 104 cannon. Her burthen tonnage is 2,162, equivalent to a displacement of about 3,560t. With a ship's company of 850 officers and ratings, HMS *Victory* served as flagship for Admirals Keppel, Hardy, Geary, Drake, Hyde Parker, Kempenfelt, Howe, Hood, Man, Linzee, Jervis, Yorke, and Saumarez, in the battles off Ushant, Gibraltar, Cape Spartel, Toulon, Calvi, Hyeres, St Vincent and Corunna, and in the Baltic. But it is as Nelson's flagship at the Battle of Trafalgar on 21 October 1805 that HMS *Victory* is most famous. Every anniversary she hoists the famous signal 'England expects that every man will do his Duty'.

In 1922 HMS *Victory* was moved into drydock in Portsmouth Dockyard. Preserved as a living memorial to Nelson and the men of the Royal Navy under sail, HMS *Victory* is still a properly-commissioned unit of the Royal Navy. She wears the White Ensign, flies the flag of the C-in-C Naval Home Command, and is manned by regular serving officers and men of the Royal Navy and the Royal Marines.

Open: Mondays-Saturdays 10.30-17.30 (16.30 November-February); Sundays 13.00-17.00 (16.30 November-February).
Closed: Christmas Day; also on certain ceremonial occasions and for official functions.
Admission: Free.
Facilities for disabled: Groups of not more than 10 people in wheelchairs may pay special visits to the Lower Gun Deck.
Nearest station: Portsmouth Harbour.

Nelson's Dockyard

Antigua; Tel 0101-809 46 31053.

A Royal Naval Dockyard at English Harbour on the Leeward Island of Antigua in the West Indies was begun in 1726. Captain Horatio Nelson was based here from 1785 to 1787, and it was here that he met and married Frances Nisbet from the nearby island of Nevis. Prince William Henry (Duke of Clarence) was there at the same time in command of the frigate HMS *Pegasus* — he later became King William IV ('The Sailor King'), and his residence in Antigua became known as Clarence House. The base itself acquired and retained the title of 'Nelson's Dockyard'. It was closed in 1889, but the buildings have now been restored and a museum opened in one of them. Its exhibits illustrate the period when the West Indies were vital to Britain's naval operations, a reminder of the ever-changing priorities of maritime strategy. Clarence House is now the country residence of the President of Antigua.

Open: 08.30-18.00
Admission: EC$1.00

The Nelson Collection

The Market Hall, Priory Street, Monmouth, Gwent. Tel (0600)-2122.

A comprehensive collection of relics and other items associated with the life and times of Lord Nelson and Lady Hamilton, plus commemorative material produced since.

Open: Mondays-Saturdays 10.30-13.00/14.00-17.00; Sundays 14.00-17.00.
Closed: Christmas Day; Boxing Day; New Year's Day.
Admission: 45p Adults; 25p Children.
Facilities for disabled: Ground Floor only (which comprises 60% of the display) plus attached Local History Museum.

Royal Naval Museum, Portsmouth

(HM Naval Base, Portsmouth, Hampshire; Tel: (0705)-822351 extn 23868/9.

For obvious security reasons, most of the Dockyard is closed to the general public, a specified route guiding visitors from the Main Gate to HMS *Victory*, the Royal Naval Museum, and the *Mary Rose*. However, even along this short distance a variety of historic features can be seen (but not photographed). There is the mast pond, where great spars and long timbers were floated to prevent their drying out and splitting while awaiting installation in sailing men o'war. The brick building (336m long) opposite HMS *Victory's* bowsprit is a ropery where rigging and cables were produced. It replaced an even earlier structure burned in 1776 by an arsonist alleged to be working for the American revolutionaries. Located farther inside the complex (and not accessible) are the blockmills, built in 1805 by Samuel Bentham and Marc Isambard Brunel. These manufactured rigging blocks — one of the earliest examples of modern mass-production, and significant in industrial archaeology as well as in maritime history. Many of these buildings are still in use as offices and stores. Advice on their modernisation, preservation or recording is provided by the Portsmouth Dockyard Preservation Society (Hon Secretary, 8 Florence Road, Southsea, Portsmouth) — which is separate from the Royal Naval Museum.

A Dockyard Museum was established in 1903-10, being opened to the public in 1911. When HMS *Victory* was preserved in drydock, a purpose-built 'Victory Gallery' was constructed nearby and opened in 1932. This developed into the Royal Naval Museum, and has recently expanded into a row of old dockyard storehouses dating from the 1780s.

The Museum now covers the whole of the period from Tudor times to the present day. There is a model of Portsmouth Dockyard, plus models of warships, relics and memorabilia of naval heroes and battles and service life from worldwide operations in the 19th and 20th centuries. Nevertheless, there is natural emphasis on HMS *Victory*, with such notable exhibits as the Trafalgar Panorama by W. L. Wyllie and the McCarthy Collection of Nelson memorabilia.

Open: Mondays-Saturdays 10.30-17.00 (16.30 November-February); Sundays 13.00-17.00 (16.30 November-February).
Closed: Christmas week.
Admission: 50p Adults; 25p Children and OAPs; £1.25 Family Ticket.
Facilities for Disabled: Ground Floors of all buildings accessible.
Nearest station: Portsmouth Harbour.

Foudroyant

Portsmouth Harbour, Hampshire.

Built of teak, HMS *Trincomalee* was laid down at Bombay Dockyard in 1816 and launched in 1817. Designed as a 5th Rate Frigate of 46 guns, she was not commissioned until 1847 — and then with only 24 cannon. After serving off America and in the Pacific for almost 10 years, she became a stationary drill-ship. Since 1897, HMS *Trincomalee* has been moored in Portsmouth Harbour as the training ship *Foudroyant*. She is now owned by a charitable trust, giving teenagers of both sexes theoretical and practical experience of basic seamanship. *Foudroyant* is not normally open to the general public, but close-up views can be obtained from 'trips round the harbour'. She measures approximately 46m×12m with a displacement of 1,470t.

Open: There is a public open day in mid-September. Tel (0705)-582696.
Closed: At all other times.
Facilities for disabled: No.
Nearest station: Portsmouth Harbour.

HMS Unicorn

Victoria Dock, Dundee, Tayside. Tel (0382)-21555.

One of the same class of frigates as HMS *Trincomalee*, HMS *Unicorn* was laid down at Chatham in 1822, and launched in 1824. She incorporates a unique blend of iron and wood construction, representing the evolutionary link between the old and new navies. However, she was never completed, and has spent her whole career as a stationary harbour vessel. From 1874 onwards she served as a drill-ship for the Tay Division of the RNR at Dundee. Nevertheless, HMS *Unicorn* has remained afloat for the whole of her life — apart from routine dockings. Although the same size as *Foudroyant*, she looks bigger because of the full-length roofed accommodation built above the main-deck. This is itself of considerable interest, and worthy of preservation because it is the only known existing example of a once-common method of protecting ships laid up in ordinary, as the reserve fleet of those days was called.

HMS *Unicorn* (the oldest British-built ship afloat), is now being restored and rigged to the condition originally intended by her designer, and can be visited by the public.

Above:
The Royal Naval Museum, Portsmouth, seen from near the bow of HMS *Victory*. *RN Museum*

Right:
As visitors approach the *Mary Rose*, HMS *Victory* and the Royal Naval Museum at Portsmouth, they pass a number of display windows. One of these exhibitions at present contains artefacts recovered from HMS *Invincible*, the first of her name, wrecked off Portsmouth in 1758. There are no plans to raise the ship herself, but the '*Invincible* (1758) Committee' is investigating and recording the site, recovering and preserving items from it. Apart from the display already mentioned, some objects are in several maritime museums. Others are housed in a mobile exhibition in a converted bus, until a permanent location is determined. At present operations are conducted from 6-10 Kirkstall Road, Southsea, Hampshire; Tel (0705) 730674. This engraving not only portrays the ship herself, but is also the emblem of the '*Invincible* (1758) Committee'.
Invincible (1758) Committee

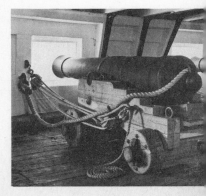

Right:
Symbolic of the Age of Fighting Sail, these smooth-bore, muzzle-loading cannon are preserved on board HMS *Unicorn* at Dundee.
Unicorn Preservation Society

112

Open: *April-October:* Mondays, Wednesdays-Saturdays 11.00-13.00/14.00-17.00; Sundays 14.00-17.00.
Closed: Tuesdays; all winter.
Admission: 50p Adults; 25p Children.
Facilities for disabled: View of exterior only.
Nearest station: Dundee.

HMS Warrior

Coal Dock, Hartlepool, Cleveland. Tel (0429)-33051. Administration at Ships Preservation Trust Ltd, The Custom House, Victoria Terrace, Hartlepool TS24 0SD.

HMS *Warrior* was built in Mare's Yard (Thames Ironworks) at Blackwall in east London. Laid down in 1859 and launched in 1860, she was completed in 1861. She had three fully-rigged masts, plus horizontal trunk steam engines driving a single propeller. HMS *Warrior* was the Royal Navy's first iron-hulled and ironclad battleship. However, like earlier vessels, her heavy muzzle-loading and new breech- loading guns were still disposed in broadsides along her clipper-bowed hull.

HMS *Warrior* served in the Victorian Navy until 1881, when she was withdrawn from sea-going operations. Her decks were eventually covered with concrete and she became an oil-fuel jetty at Pembroke Dock.

Recently it was proposed that she should be preserved as a fitting representative of the Victorian ironclads, and as a link between the old sailing men o'war and modern warships. She was towed to Hartlepool Coal Dock, where the work of restoration can be seen in progress.

It is hoped that in 1986, HMS *Warrior* will be permanently berthed at Portsmouth. A dock is being prepared alongside the Common Hard and outside the Main Gate, but only accessible from within the dockyard complex.

HMS *Warrior* is about 119m long and displaces approximately 9,250t.

Open: *Easter-August:* Saturdays, Sundays and Bank Holidays 14.00-17.00.
Closed: Mondays-Fridays; all winter.
Admission: 70p Adults; 40p Children and OAPs; £2.00 Family Ticket.
Facilities for disabled: View of exterior only.
Nearest station: Hartlepool.

HMS Gannet

Fareham Creek, Portsmouth Harbour, Hampshire.
Administration: c/o Muffins, Forest Rise, Liss Forest, Hampshire. Tel 0730 892303.

The mere existence of mighty battleships like HMS *Warrior* provided an impressive shield behind which the Empire and its trade could prosper. But most of the routine anti-piracy and anti-slavery patrols, showing-the-flag visits, and the provision of landing parties for punitive expeditions, was carried out by smaller warships, such as steam gunboats measuring 52m and displacing 1,150t.

HMS *Gannet* is just such a vessel. She is still afloat, owned by the Maritime Trust and administered by the HMS *Gannet* (1878) Society. She is being preserved as a typical representative of the day of 'Send-a-Gunboat' diplomacy. Built at Sheerness in 1878, she served in the Red Sea in 1888, her arrival relieving Kitchener's Army besieged in Suakin. From 1910 to 1968 she served as an accommodation ship for a nautical training school under the name of *Mercury*. When reconstructed with masts, rigging and much of her interior equipment, she will be open to the public in the Gosport area. At present only the exterior of her hull can be viewed from 'trips round the harbour' boats.

Nearest station: Portsmouth Harbour.

RRS Discovery

Historic Ship Collection/Maritime Trust, East Basin, St Katharine's Dock, London, E1. Tel 01-481 0043.

The St Katharine's Dock complex was designed by Thomas Telford in 1824-28. It is now the home of a variety of historic vessels including a tug, a lightship, a coaster and a sailing barge. Among them is *Discovery*, built for the National Antarctic Expedition of 1901-04 under Commander Robert Falcon Scott. A magnetic observatory and other scientific equipment fitted her for the investigation and recording of every aspect of polar exploration including meteorology, hydrography and marine biology. In addition, she acted as an ice-bound base-ship for sledging expeditions into the interior. Returning from the expedition, *Discovery* continued to be employed in polar seas, but outside the Service. In 1937 she became a training vessel for the Sea Scouts and the wartime RN. From 1955 to 1979 she was attached to the RNR London Division, being known as '*HMS*' *Discovery*. However, her formal title is a 'Royal Research Ship'. She displaces 1,700t and is 70m long. RRS *Discovery* is now restored by the Maritime Trust, a charity devoted to the conservation and study of Britain's sea-going heritage.

Open: Daily 10.00-17.00.
Closed: Christmas Day, New Year's Day.
Admission to whole of complex: £1.60p Adults; 80p Children and OAPs.
Facilities for disabled: View from quayside only.
Nearest stations: Tower Hill, Fenchurch Street.

Naval Ordnance Museum

Priddy's Hard, Gosport, Hampshire. Tel 0705-822351, ext 44225.

Within the extended historic setting of an 18th century Board of Ordnance gunpowder magazine, this museum displays the history of ordnance and its administration from its earliest days. Exhibits show many examples of shot and shell of all types, from smooth bore cannon, rifled muzzle-loading guns to later and modern breech-loaders, with many of the guns themselves also on display. The torpedo collection, of early and modern examples, is the largest in the country; various sea mines, anti-submarine weapons, aircraft bombs, guns and missiles are also exhibited, and a fine collection of small arms from countries worldwide may be seen in the Armoury. Photographic and printed wall displays complement the many exhibits, and a large archive collection of gun and ammunition handbooks, gun registers and Ordnance

Above:
HMS *Gannet* in Fareham Creek at the top end of Portsmouth Harbour on 8 August 1984. *Author*

Left:
Looking aft from the forecastle of the RRS *Discovery* in St Katharine's Dock, London, on 12 May 1984. *Author*

Below:
The Naval Ordnance Museum, Priddy's Hard, Gosport.
Naval Ordnance Museum

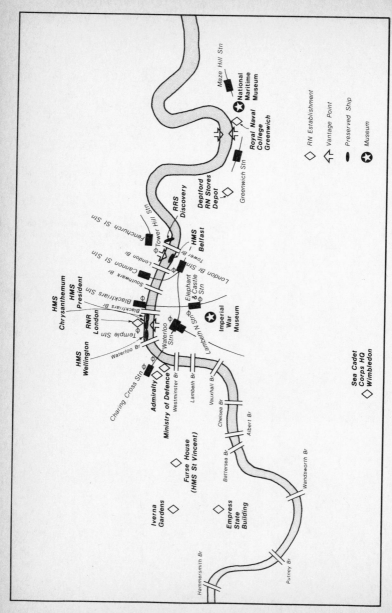

Hammersmith Br
Putney Br
Wandsworth Br
Albert Br
Chelsea Br
Battersea Br
Vauxhall Br
Lambeth Br
Westminster Br
Charing Cross Stn
Waterloo Br
Waterloo Stn
Lambeth N Stn
Blackfriars Br
Blackfriars Stn
Temple Stn
Southwark Br
Cannon St Stn
London Br Stn
London Br
Elephant & Castle Stn
Tower Hill Stn
Fenchurch St Stn
Greenwich Stn
Maze Hill Stn

Iverna Gardens
Empress State Building
Furse House (HMS St Vincent)
Ministry of Defence
Admiralty
HMS Wellington
HMS Chrysanthemum
HMS President
RNR London
Imperial War Museum
HMS Belfast
RRS Discovery
Deptford RN Stores Depot
Royal Naval College Greenwich
National Maritime Museum
Sea Cadet Corps HQ Wimbledon

◇ RN Establishment
⚓ Vantage Point
▬ Preserved Ship
✪ Museum

116

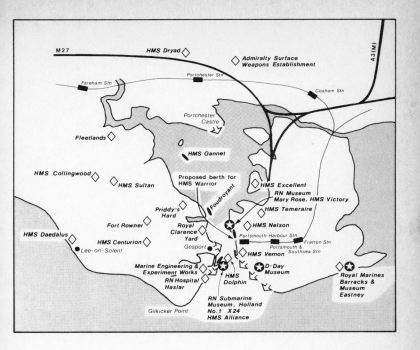

business letters dating from 1695 is available to museum staff as a valuable reference source.

Access to the museum is provided by conducted tours; providing a week or more of notice is given, parties of 6-15 persons are given a tour of approximately 1½ hours, upon application to the Curator.

Royal Naval Medical Museum

Royal Naval Hospital, Haslar, Gosport, Hampshire. Tel 0705-584255, ext 2335.

This Museum covers the history of the Royal Naval Medical Service through the centuries, particularly the 18th and 19th. There is also a collection of books on Natural History and Exploration.

The Royal Naval Medical Museum has a restricted entry and is not normally open to the general public; however, individuals with special interests and organised groups are sometimes admitted by prior arrangement and the permission of The Medical Officer in Charge. It is possible that the collection will be made more accessible at some time in the future.

117

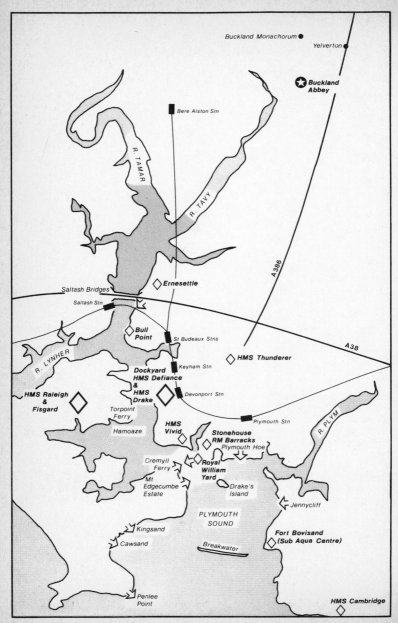

Buckland Monachorum •

Yelverton •

★ **Buckland Abbey**

■ Bere Alston Stn

R. TAMAR

R. TAVY

A 386

◇ **Ernesettle**

Saltash Bridges

■ Saltash Stn

◇ **Bull Point**

■ St Budeaux Stns

◇ **HMS Thunderer**

A 38

R. LYNHER

■ Keyham Stn

Dockyard HMS Defiance & HMS Drake

◇

■ Devonport Stn

HMS Raleigh & Fisgard

◇

Torpoint Ferry

HMS Vivid

◇

Stonehouse RM Barracks

Plymouth Hoe

■ Plymouth Stn

R. PLYM

Hamoaze

Cremyll Ferry

◇ **Royal William Yard**

Drake's Island

Mt Edgecumbe Estate

PLYMOUTH SOUND

Jennycliff

Kingsand

Cawsand

Breakwater

Fort Bovisand (Sub Aqua Centre)

◇

Penlee Point

HMS Cambridge ◇

Trecwn

Nelson Collection
Monmouth

Milford Haven

Pembroke
Dock

Llangennech

RNR South Wales

Cardiff

RNR Severn

Bristol

Bath

Bridgwater
Admiral Blake Museum

FAA Museum

Taunton
(Hydrographic
Department)

Yeovilton
(HMS Heron)

Exeter

Lympstone

Portland
(HMS
Osprey)

PLYMOUTH
AREA

Dartmouth
(RNC
Britannia)

Cornwall Aero Park

Culdrose
(HMS Seahawk)

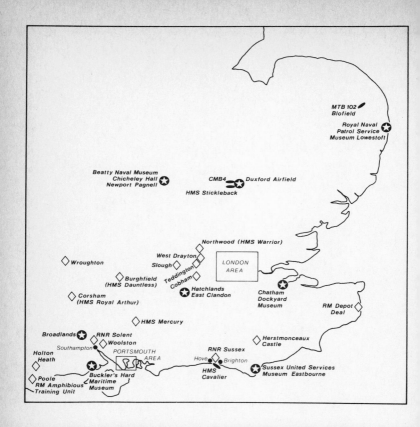

Map showing locations including: MTB 102 Blofield; Royal Naval Patrol Service Museum Lowestoft; Beatty Naval Museum Chicheley Hall Newport Pagnell; CMB4 Duxford Airfield; HMS Stickleback; Northwood (HMS Warrior); Wroughton; West Drayton; Slough; Teddington; Burghfield (HMS Dauntless); Cobham; Corsham (HMS Royal Arthur); Hatchlands East Clandon; LONDON AREA; Chatham Dockyard Museum; RM Depot Deal; HMS Mercury; Broadlands; RNR Solent; Woolston; Southampton; PORTSMOUTH AREA; Herstmonceaux Castle; RNR Sussex; Hove; Brighton; Holton Heath; Poole RM Amphibious Training Unit; Buckler's Hard Maritime Museum; HMS Cavalier; Sussex United Services Museum Eastbourne

Royal Navy Submarine Museum

Haslar Pontoon Road, Gosport, Hampshire PO12 2AB. Tel 0705-29217.

HMS *Dolphin* is the official title for the Royal Navy's first submarine base to be established in 1905 in Fort Blockhouse, one of the old forts built to defend the entrance to Portsmouth Harbour. The base is still very much operational, and the Alma Mater of all British submarines. Standing just outside the perimeter (so that visitors can come and go, without the particular security problems associated with the base itself) is situated the Royal Navy Submarine Museum. Models, relics and photographs cover the history of underwater warfare from the earliest submersibles (such as Bushnell's *Turtle* of 1776) to modern nuclear-powered and missile-firing submarines. It is naturally most concerned with the Royal Navy, but there is also reference to developments and operations in other navies. There are complete weapons, technical displays, cartoons, paintings, medals and personal memorabilia. One of the most poignant exhibits is an unopened bottle of whisky, won in a raffle by a submariner setting out on patrol, who never returned to claim his prize. The Museum's exhibits include three actual submarines: *Holland I*, *X24* and *Alliance*.

Open: Daily 09.30-16.30.
Closed: Christmas Eve; Christmas Day.
Admission: Free (but charge for HMS *Alliance* and *Holland I*); Car park 30p (coaches free).
Facilities for disabled: Ground floor only.
Nearest station: Portsmouth Harbour via Gosport Ferry. At some times of the year, there is also a special ferry service linking the historic ships in Portsmouth Harbour — look for signs on Portsmouth Hard.

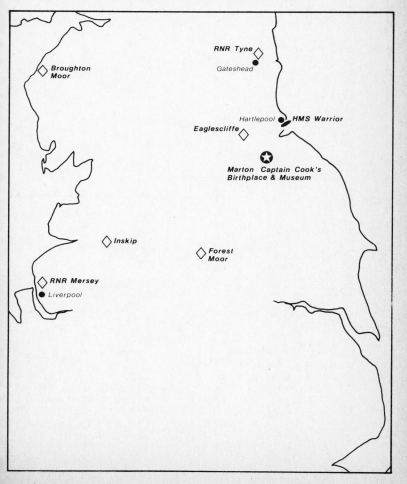

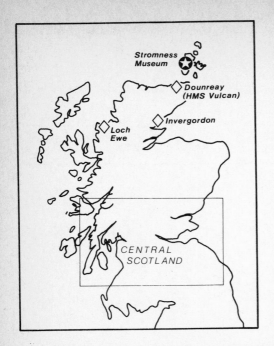

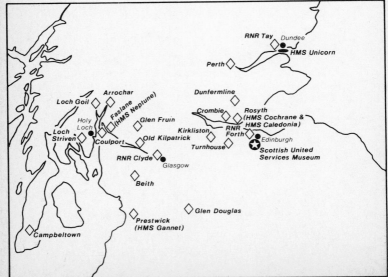

Holland I

Royal Navy Submarine Museum, Haslar Pontoon Road, Gosport, Hampshire PO12 2AB. Tel 0705-529217.

The Royal Navy's first submarine, launched in 1901, *Holland I* is 19.3m long with a displacement of 106t. A temperamental petrol engine gave her a surface speed of 7kt, and she was armed with a single 18-inch (45.7cm) torpedo-tube. By 1913 *Holland I* had been totally eclipsed by such boats as the comparatively reliable 'E' class, six times as big and with five torpedo-tubes. *Holland I* was towed away to be scrapped, but en route the crewless vessel foundered off Plymouth. Her precise location forgotten, *Holland I* was relocated in 1981 and raised the following year. Now she is being restored at the RN Submarine Museum. Although small by today's standards, *Holland I* is still much bigger than one expects, and doors are being cut in her side so that visitors can view her interior.

Opening times, etc are the same as the Royal Navy Submarine Museum, namely:

Open: Daily 09.30-16.30.
Closed: Christmas Eve; Christmas Day.
Admission: Free (until restoration is complete when there will be an admission charge); Car park 30p (coaches free).
Facilities for disabled: View exterior only.
Nearest station: Portsmouth Harbour via Gosport Ferry. At some times of the year, there is also a special ferry service linking the historic ships in Portsmouth Harbour — look for signs on Portsmouth Hard.

Fleet Air Arm Museum

Royal Naval Air Station, Yeovilton, Somerset. Tel 0935-840565.

Located just off the A303 on the approach road to the village of Ilchester, this Museum covers the whole history of British naval aviation from the appointment of a Naval Air Assistant at the Admiralty in 1908. There are models of airships, carriers and aeroplanes, dioramas of actual events, photographs and diagrams, all describing development and operations in two world wars and other conflicts. There are mementoes, details of FAA personalities and an art gallery depicting the beauty and harshness of flight over the sea.

Most memorable are the naval aircraft themselves, more than 40 of them dating from a World War 1 Sopwith Camel to modern jets; there is also the fuselage of the Short 184 Seaplane which flew at the Battle of Jutland in 1916. Some (like the Blackburn Skua) have been recovered from beneath the water. Others (like the Sea Gladiator) have been totally restored. What is most impressive of them all is their size. They may look small in photographs of carrier flight-decks, but the Corsair, Avenger and Walrus were very big aircraft indeed, considering they were only single-engined machines. Other aircraft on view include a Sopwith Baby, Fulmar, Martlet, Hellcat, Seafire, Sea Vampire, Attacker, Skyraider, Wyvern, Seahawk, Sea Venom, Scimitar, Sea Vixen, Gannet, Buccaneer, Sea Prince, Meteor and the Hiller, Whirlwind, P531, Dragonfly and Wessex helicopters.

A new section tells the story of the Japanese kamikazes, while history is

Above:
Work in progress on the preservation of *Holland I* at the Royal Navy Submarine Museum, Gosport, on 8 August 1984. *Author*

Below:
A view of the entrance to the Fleet Air Arm Museum at Yeovilton in Somerset. A Blackburn Buccaneer stands in front of the staircase approach, while through the big glass windows can be glimpsed a Sopwith Baby seaplane, a Bleriot Monoplane and the nose of Concorde 002. On the extreme right of the photograph, beyond the de Havilland Sea Vixen, are the runways of the Royal Naval Air Station HMS *Heron*. *Author*

Bottom:
Spring sunshine glints on the breech mechanisms of the 15in guns outside the Imperial War Museum in London. *Author*

brought up to date with the Falklands Exhibition — the largest permanent display relating to this conflict in the country, including four captured Argentine aircraft.

The Concorde 002 Museum is located alongside the Fleet Air Arm Museum in its own Exhibition Hall. Outside, the visitor can see aircraft of the modern Navy taking off from and landing on the runways of HMS *Heron*.

A Swordfish, Firefly and Sea Fury, are still maintained in flying condition by HMS *Heron*'s Historic Flight. They can be seen at many air displays in the South of England during the summer (including Yeovilton's own air show, which is usually held in August).

Open: Daily 10.00-17.30 (16.30 winter).
Closed: Christmas Eve; Christmas Day.
Admission: £1.70 Adults; 85p Children and OAPs.
Facilities for disabled: Fully accessible.

Imperial War Museum

Lambeth Road, London SE1 6HZ. Tel 01-735 8922.

Founded during World War 1 as a 'Memorial of Effort and Sacrifice', the Imperial War Museum eventually moved to what was originally the Bethlem Hospital in Lambeth. The museum's terms of reference have been extended to include all operations in which Commonwealth forces have been engaged since 1914. In effect, it covers every aspect of the influence of war on international society during the 20th century.

The Royal Navy is but one of the factors in those events, and as such receives appropriate consideration. However, the approach to the building is dominated by two 15inch (38.1cm) naval guns, representatives of the mighty arbiters of dreadnought seapower. One came from the battleship HMS *Resolution* and the other from her sister-ship, HMS *Ramillies*. This latter saw action at the Battle of Cape Spartivento in 1940. It was subsequently mounted in the monitor HMS *Roberts* for bombardment during the landings in Normandy and on Walcheren in 1944.

The exhibits inside the museum, include an Italian human torpedo, a German Biber one-man submarine, and Jack Cornwell's VC, won at the Battle of Jutland.

Open: Mondays-Saturdays, 10.00-17.50, Sundays 14.00-17.50.
Closed: New Year's Day; Good Friday; May Day; Christmas Eve; Christmas Day; Boxing Day.
Admission: Free.
Facilities for disabled: Fully accessible.
Nearest station: Waterloo, Lambeth North, Elephant & Castle.

Beatty Naval Museum

Chicheley Hall, Newport Pagnell, Buckinghamshire, located on the A422, two miles east of Newport Pagnell and 11 miles west of Bedford. Tel (023065)-252.

Built in 1719-23, Chicheley Hall is now the home of the Beatty family. Its most famous member was Admiral of the Fleet Sir David Beatty, whose naval

Above:
The room in Chicheley Hall known as Lord Beatty's study. *Chicheley Hall*

Left:
A beer mug recovered from the German warships scuttled in Scapa Flow (now in Stromness Museum). *Orkney Natural History Museum*

Below:
The view from Blackfriars Bridge on 6 August 1983. Left to right: HMS *Wellington*; HMS *Chrysanthemum* (with a 'Ton' class MCMV alongside); and HMS *President*. *Author*

career included action in the Sudan and China. During World War 1 he commanded the Battlecruiser Fleet at the Battle of Heligoland, Dogger Bank and Jutland. Later C-in-C of the Grand Fleet, he subsequently became First Sea Lord. Chicheley Hall contains an exhibition of naval paintings, relics and memorabilia relating to his life and to the Great War at sea.

Open: *Good Friday-1 October:* Sundays and Bank Holidays 14.30-18.00.
Closed: At all other times and all winter (but parties at any time by appointment).
Admission: £1.60 Adults; 90p Children.
Facilities for disabled: Ground Floor of house only (not museum, which is on top floor).

HMS Caroline

RNR Ulster Division, Belfast.

The three-funnelled light cruiser HMS *Caroline* was completed by Cammell Laird at Birkenhead in 1914. She spent the whole of her wartime career with the Grand Fleet and is now the sole remaining survivor of the Battle of Jutland. Originally mounting four single 6in (15.2cm) guns, she was disarmed in 1926 and adapted as an RNVR drillship, performing this duty ever since. She is not open to the general public but can be viewed from alongside her berth on the River Lagan docks. HMS *Caroline* is 136m long and displaces 3,810t.

Stromness Museum

52 Alfred Street, Stromness, Orkney. Tel (0856)-246.

Although principally a museum of local history, geology and natural history, there is a section devoted to the employment of Scapa Flow as a Royal Navy base during two world wars. It also tells the story of the scuttling of the German High Seas Fleet as in 1919 and its subsequent salvage, through a growing collection of artefacts and photographs.

Open: Mondays-Wednesdays, Fridays-Saturdays 11.00-12.30/13.30-17.00; Thursdays 11.00-13.00. July-August, Opens at 10.00.
Closed: Thursdays pm; Sundays; Christmas Day, etc; three weeks in February.
Admission: 20p Adults; 5p Children.
Facilities for disabled: Ground floor access only.

HMS President

Victoria Embankment, London, EC4.

While the great battlefleets of Britain and Germany faced each other across the North Sea, U-boats and mines were causing severe losses among Allied merchant shipping in the Atlantic and Mediterranean. Typical of the 'Flower' class sloops built as minesweepers and convoy escorts was HMS *Saxifrage*, launched in 1918. She was given mercantile appearance to confuse the enemy, with the possibility of acting as a mystery Q-ship. After World War 1 HMS *Saxifrage* was renamed HMS *President* to become the nominal base ship of the Admiralty in London. She also served as a stationary training vessel for the RNR, a role which she still performs today. Not open to the public, HMS *President* can be viewed from both sides of the River Thames between Waterloo and Southwark Bridges.

Nearest stations: Waterloo, Embankment, Temple, Blackfriars.

HMS Chrysanthemum

Victoria Embankment, London EC4.

A sistership of HMS *President*, she was launched in 1917 and followed a similar career. They are both 80m long and displace 1,310t. Originally mounting two 4in (10.2cm) guns, they were both disarmed, their main engines removed and extra accommodation installed above and below decks. HMS *Chrysanthemum* is not open to the public, but can be viewed from both banks of the River Thames between Southwark and Waterloo Bridges.

Nearest stations: Waterloo, Embankment, Temple, Blackfriars.

CMB4

Duxford Airfield, Cambridgeshire CB2 4QR. Tel (0223)-833963. An out-station of the Imperial War Museum on the A505 off the M11.

Coastal motor boats were developed by Thornycroft during World War 1. Built of wood, they were intended for the defence of the approaches to British harbours, and for offensive employment against shipping in restricted waters off the enemy's coasts. *CMB4* is 12.2m long and belongs to the '40-foot' class. A petrol engine driving a single propeller gave her a top speed of 34-37kt. Her main armament was a single 18in (45.7cm) torpedo, launched tail-first over the stern, the CMB then swerving off to one side.

In 1919 *CMB4* was used by secret agents in Russia during operations against the Bolsheviks. Then, during the dark hours of 17 June 1919, *CMB4* stealthily entered Kronstadt harbour and torpedoed the Bolshevik cruiser *Oleg* — an exploit which earned Lt Augustus Agar the Victoria Cross. *CMB4* was eventually deleted from Navy lists, but was later found, refurbished by shipbuilding industry trainees, and can now be seen at Duxford Airfield. Her history and that of CMBs in general is related in photographs, diagrams and audio-visual display.

Open: *17 March-4 November:* Daily 11.00-17.30 (16.45 from 21 October).
Closed: Good Friday; May Day; All winter.
Admission: (to whole public area of the complex) £1.50 Adults; 80p Children and OAPs.
Facilities for disabled: Fully accessible.

HMS Wellington

Victoria Embankment, London EC4.

The World War 1 'Flower' class sloops proved so effective that their basic design was developed between the wars into a series of classes which, though generally similar in appearance, could be used for escort or minesweeping, or for showing the flag, patrolling and surveying in distant corners of the Empire. Those intended for service in the tropics were usually painted white. Although corvettes were later introduced specifically for convoy escort, it was soon learned that larger hulls, armament and engines were needed, and subsequent wartime construction returned to the sloop idea. These later vessels were known as 'frigates' and became the basis for almost all postwar surface warship development except aircraft-carriers.

HMS *Wellington* was an interwar sloop launched at Devonport in 1934, being originally armed with two 4.7in (11.9cm) guns. She was disarmed after the war and adapted as the stationary Headquarters ship of the Honourable Company of Master Mariners. Displacing 1,000t and 81m long, HMS *Wellington* can be viewed from both sides of the River Thames between Waterloo and Southwark Bridges. She is not open to the public.

Nearest stations: Waterloo, Temple, Embankment, Blackfriars.

MTB102

'102 Trust', 2 Church Road, Blofield, Norwich, Norfolk NR13 4NA. Tel (0603)-712262.

As World War 2 approached, naval officers and shipbuilders began to consider what new weaponry and ships would be likely to be employed in the anticipated conflict. One of the results of such deliberation was *Motor Torpedo Boat No 102*. Designed by Commander Peter Du Cane, constructed of wood by Vosper, and completed in 1937, her dimensions were 20.7m×4.5m×1m. *MTB102* had a displacement of 32.5t and a maximum speed of 48kt light, produced by three Isotta Fraschini petrol engines. Originally built as a private venture, *MTB102* was commissioned in the RN and used for the experimental installation of various types of armament. These included the 20mm Oerlikon gun, whose introduction was being advocated by Captain Lord Louis Mountbatten.

MTB102's war service included the Dunkirk evacuation (when she wore the flag of Admiral Wake-Walker). In 1943, she was transferred to the Army, temporarily renamed *Vimy*, and used for target-towing for coastal artillery practice. In 1944 *MTB102/Vimy* carried Winston Churchill and General Eisenhower on a review of the ships gathered in the Solent for the Normandy landings.

Many Coastal Forces craft were sold off at the end of the war for conversion to houseboats and private motor yachts. One such was *MTB253*, built by J. S. White of Cowes. Under the name *Medyna*, she can still be seen attending naval and military reunions and other functions. However, *Medyna's* internal fittings are completely civilian in character, unlike *MTB102*.

Admittedly *MTB102* did spend the postwar years as a private motor cruiser, being fitted with two Perkins diesels. But in 1973 she was purchased by the 1st Blofield & Brundall Scouts in Norfolk. They intended refurbishing her in wartime condition as a fully operational seagoing vessel. Three years later their hopes were fulfilled; Kelso Films agreed to undertake the work so that *MTB102* could appear in the film *The Eagle Has Landed*. Now returned, *MTB102* serves as a Sea Scout Training Ship, enabling young people of both sexes to gain practical experience of coastal navigation, communications

Above:
CMB4 at Duxford airfield, on 22 July 1984. *Author*

Right:
MTB102 at speed during her Royal Navy service. (From an original oil painting by Hubert H. Beavis, in aid of the '102 Trust'.)

Below:
HMS Belfast in the Pool of London. *Imperial War Museum*

and seamanship. She also participates in Service reunions and has twice visited Portsmouth Navy Days.

MTB102 requires constant refit and expenditure to be maintained in a sea-going condition; and when she is eventually too old for that she will be preserved on shore. Like all organisations (even national museums) preserving and restoring Royal Navy warships, aircraft and other memorabilia, the '102 Trust' welcomes donations and offers of technical and other assistance.

MTB102 is frequently open to the public during her visits to ports for special functions.

HMS Belfast

Symons' Wharf, Vine Lane, off Tooley Street, London SE1 2JH. Tel: (01)-407 6434.

At 11,700t displacement and 186m long, HMS *Belfast* is the Royal Navy's largest cruiser, and is as typical of her day as HMS *Victory* is of the sailing-ship Navy.

HMS *Belfast* was launched in 1938 and commissioned in time to take part in the opening moves of World War 2. She captured the largest prize ever taken on the high seas (the German liner *Cap Norte*), but was so badly damaged by a magnetic mine that she spent almost three years in dockyard hands. Repairs complete, she provided cover for Russian convoys. On Boxing Day 1943, she participated in the Royal Navy's last gun battle between capital ships, when the German battlecruiser *Scharnhorst* was sunk. D-Day, 6 June 1944, saw HMS *Belfast*'s 12 6in (15.2cm) guns pounding enemy positions during the Allied landings in Normandy. Her postwar activities included service in the Korean War. In 1960 HMS *Belfast* was modernised for operations in the electronic and nuclear age, and was eventually preserved as a museum ship in 1971.

Although her occasional movements to and from drydock have to be under tow, HMS *Belfast* is still a living ship. The White Ensign Association, the City of London Sea Cadet Corps Unit, and the Royal Naval Amateur Radio Association all have offices or otherwise meet regularly on board. The Admiral's Quarters, Wardroom, Wardroom Ante-Room and the Ship's Company Dining Room can be hired for private functions, including meals (details from the Catering Manager on (01)-403 6246). Warships of all nations berth outboard alongside HMS *Belfast* when visiting the Pool of London. These vessels are sometimes open to members of the public, details being available from HMS *Belfast* (the normal admission charge for the latter being payable).

On board HMS *Belfast* herself, at least one compartment in each department of the ship is open; from the director-control-tower on top of the bridge, to the machinery spaces below; and from the cells forward to the quarterdeck aft. Some compartments show how accommodation and equipment have altered during the ship's career, while others are employed as exhibition galleries. 'The Cruiser Museum', 'Ships' Crests', 'Battleships', 'Naval Gunnery' and 'North Cape' are but five of the permanent and temporary displays in this out-station of the Imperial War Museum.

Open: Daily 11.00-17.50 (16.30 winter).

Closed: New Year's Day; Good Friday; May Day; Christmas Eve; Christmas Day; Boxing Day.
Admission: £2 Adults; £1 Children and OAPs (concessions for students and unemployed).
Facilities for disabled: View from quayside.
Nearest stations: London Bridge (walk along Tooley Street), Tower Hill and Fenchurch Street (walk over Tower Bridge or ferry from Tower Pier — the latter operates daily in summer, weekends in winter).

Royal Naval Patrol Service Museum

Sparrow's Nest, Lowestoft, Suffolk NR32 1XG. Tel (0502)-86250.

As in the Great War, so too in 1939-45 a great deal of action was seen by the little ships. Many of them were mercantile vessels requisitioned or purchased by the RN. Trawlers, drifters and whalers — their fish-holds converted into accommodation spaces and magazines — were particularly suitable. They were employed as anti-submarine escorts, boom defence vessels, harbour ferries, torpedo recovery vessels, target-tugs, small-craft depot-ships, wreck dispersal vessels, degaussing vessels, tank cleaning vessels, store-carriers, mooring vessels, buoy tenders, controlled minelayers, barrage balloon vessels, mine recovery vessels, auxiliary patrol craft, submarine tenders, harbour defence craft, contraband control examination vessels, water-carriers, hospital ships, coastal tankers, firefloats, flare and smokescreen craft, air-sea rescue vessels, salvage craft, radar pickets, training ships, netlayers and experimental vessels. Above all there was minesweeping. The same stretch of water had to be covered over and over again — often without result just in case one single mine had been missed, or had been fitted with a delay mechanism to activate it long after repeated sweeping had apparently made the channel safe.

Later in the war purpose-built motor-minesweepers were completed in both Britain and America, while some yards delivered vessels of fishing-craft design which could be sold by the Admiralty for easy conversion into commercial trawlers when peace came.

All these activities are described at the Royal Naval Patrol Service Museum, housed in what was the organisation's Central Depot, officially known as HMS *Europa*. The Museum includes exhibits relating to Lieutenant Richard Stannard RNR who won the VC in HMS *Arab* at Namsos in Norway in 1940. But the display is not restricted to the famous. The Museum welcomes visits from, and news of, any of the 70,000 officers and ratings who manned the RNPS during the war — and after, for minesweeping continued long after the official end of hostilities. (Indeed, all preserved ships and naval branch museums are pleased to meet former members of their ships' companies.)

Open: *May-October:* Daily 10.00-12.00/14.00-16.30.
Closed: Winter.
Admission: Free.
Nearest station: Lowestoft.

Malta National War Museum

Fort St Elmo, Valletta.

Fort St Elmo was built by the Knights of St John in the 16th century. Its position dominates the approaches to Grand Harbour and Marsamuxetto Harbour (which includes Sliema Creek). Fort St Elmo put up a valiant defence before being overwhelmed by the Turks during the Great Siege of Malta in 1565, but eventually the Turkish army and fleet was forced to withdraw. Fort St Elmo played its part in the defence and administration of Malta during subsequent centuries, and on the night of 26/27 July 1941 its coastal artillery helped to beat off an attack by Italian explosive motor-boats. It is therefore appropriate that Fort St Elmo should now be the home of Malta's National War Museum.

The Museum tells the whole story of the George Cross Island during World War 2, including sections on civilian life, anti-aircraft defence and the RAF. Torpedoes, badges, photographs, models and relics describe the Royal Navy's part in the convoys vital to Malta's survival, and in the surface submarine and aerial striking forces which so hindered the flow of Axis supplies to the North African desert.

Open: *16 June-30 September:* 07.45-14.00; *10 October-15 June:* 08.15-17.00.
Closed: Public holidays.
Admission: 15 cents Adults; 7 cents 5 mils Children.
Facilities for disabled: Museum is located on the ground floor of Fort St Elmo.

X24

RN Submarine Museum, Haslar Pontoon Road, Gosport, Hampshire PO12 2AB. Tel (0705)-529217.

X-craft (or midget submarines) were developed during World War 2. They were intended for stealthy assault on targets in heavily-defended harbours in waters too restricted for penetration by conventionally-sized boats. X-craft varied in length from 15.2 to 16.4m with a displacement of 27-37t. Each carried a crew of four, including a frogman-diver, who left and entered the submarine via a floodable wet-and-dry compartment. It was his task to cut a way through defensive nets and attach limpet mines to the hull of the target. At the same time the X-craft could release two massive containers of high-explosive (or side-cargoes) which lay on the seabed under the enemy vessel, lifting her bodily with lethal effect when they detonated.

X24 (unofficially named HMS *Expeditious*) was twice towed across the North Sea by a parent submarine, HMS *Sceptre*. On each occasion *X24* slipped her tow offshore and entered Bergen harbour. As a result of these two attacks (on 14 April and 11 September 1944), the German freighter *Barenfels* and a floating dock were sunk, two other ships damaged, and a coaling wharf wrecked.

X24 survived the war and has been preserved at the Royal Navy Submarine Museum at Gosport, along with *Holland I* and HMS *Alliance*. Too cramped for public entry, she has been sectioned so that visitors can see inside her.

Opening times, etc are the same as the Royal Navy Submarine Museum, namely:

Open: Daily 09.30-16.30.
Closed: Christmas Day.
Admission: Free (car park 30p, coaches free).
Facilities for disabled: View exterior only.
Nearest station: Portsmouth Harbour via Gosport Ferry. At some times of the year, there is also a special ferry service linking the historic ships in Portsmouth Harbour (look for signs at Portsmouth Hard).

D-Day Museum

Clarence Esplanade, Portsmouth, Hampshire. Tel (0705)-827261.

The museum houses the Overlord Embroidery consisting of 34 panels measuring a total of 83m. It tells the story of the Allied return to Europe, beginning with the summer of 1940 and ending with victory in the Battle of Normandy in August 1944. A multi-language audio-visual presentation describes the debates about, the preparation for, and the action during, the assault.

In a separate section are guns, tanks and DUKWs, and other three-dimensional exhibits, dioramas, models, photographs and diagrams illustrating the most famous successful amphibious operation of modern times. The Navy's part in the assault and build-up (officially codenamed Operation 'Neptune') is fully represented and includes a full-sized reconstruction of part of the room containing the D-Day plot in Southwick House (itself part of HMS *Dryad* shore establishment and usually closed to the general public).

Open: Daily 10.30-17.30.
Closed: Christmas Eve; Christmas Day; Boxing Day.
Admission: £1.25 Adults; 75p Children and OAPs. This includes admission to Southsea Castle, from whose ramparts, Henry VIII witnessed the sinking of the *Mary Rose*.
Facilities for disabled: Fully accessible (wheelchairs available) plus facilities for hard of hearing.
Nearest station: Portsmouth & Southsea.

HMS Cavalier

Brighton Marina, Brighton, Sussex BN2 5UF.

HMS *Cavalier* was launched by J. S. White of Cowes on 7 April 1944 and completed in November of that year. She is 120.5m long and displaces 2,550t full load. HMS *Cavalier* served on Russian convoys at the end of World War 2 and then took part in a variety of postwar operations. These included the pacification of Java in November 1945, the atom-bomb tests at Christmas Island in 1957, the Brunei rebellion of 1962 and the Beira patrol in the 1960s, as well as various NATO and SEATO exercises. She survived a 1964 collision with the tanker *Burean* and herself salvaged the coaster *Saint Brendon* in 1970. Laid up in 1972, HMS *Cavalier* was purchased by the HMS *Cavalier* Trust to be preserved as a typical representative of the 1,054 destroyer-type vessels which have served in the Royal Navy. At first she was berthed at Southampton, but she is now at Brighton Marina. Her existing armament comprises three 4.5in (11.4cm) guns, two 40mm anti-aircraft guns, two triple

Squid anti-submarine mortars, and a quadruple Seacat anti-aircraft missile launcher. A shipboard display illustrating the history of destroyers in the Royal Navy is being prepared.

Open: Daily at 10.30 (closing time varies according to the time of year).
Closed: Christmas Eve; Christmas Day; Boxing Day.
Admission: £1.50 Adults; 80p Children and OAPs. *Car visitors:* parking fee plus £1.20 Adults and 70p Children.
Nearest station: Brighton.

HMS Alliance

Royal Navy Submarine Museum, Haslar Pontoon Road, Gosport, Hampshire. Tel (0705)-529217.

The submarine HMS *Alliance* was launched by Vickers Armstrong at Barrow-in-Furness in 1945. Intended for service in the Pacific, the war ended before she saw action. In 1958-60 she was modernised and streamlined, her squat, gun-armed conning-tower being replaced by a tall 'fin' or 'sail'. Her main armament now comprised six 21in (53.3cm) torpedo-tubes, and she displaced 1,410t. Her 86.8m length accommodated 68 officers and ratings. Her diesel engines gave her a surfaced speed of 18kt, while her electric motors drove her submerged at 10kt. Reducing speed to 2½kt gave her an underwater endurance of 36 hours, but by then the air would have become extremely foul. The use of snort equipment made things a little better for conventional submarines, but modern nuclear boats are able to recycle breathable air and can stay submerged indefinitely.

In 1978 HMS *Alliance* was transferred on permanent loan to the Royal Navy Submarine Museum. She has been raised out of the water, thus easing conservation. Two doors have been cut in her side for public access. An audio-visual presentation tells visitors about her before they are taken on a guided tour of the boat. HMS *Alliance* is not only the Royal Navy Submarine Museum's largest exhibit, she is also a memorial to the 5,073 officers and ratings lost in British submarines in peace and war.

The opening times are the same as for the Royal Navy Submarine Museum, namely:

Open: 09.30-16.30 daily.
Closed: Christmas Eve; Christmas Day.
Admission: £1.80 Adults; 90p Children; 30p Car park (coaches free).
Facilities for disabled: View of exterior only.
Nearest station: Portsmouth Harbour via Gosport Ferry. At some times of the year, there is also a special ferry service linking the historic ships in Portsmouth Harbour — look for signs on Portsmouth Hard.

HMS Stickleback

Duxford Airfield, Cambridgeshire CB2 4QR. Tel (0223)-833963. An out-station of the Imperial War Museum on the A505 off the M11.

Officially designated *X51*, HMS *Stickleback* was launched in 1954. From 1958 onwards she served in the Royal Swedish Navy, but she eventually returned to Britain and is now on display at Duxford Airfield. Though a

Left:
A close-up of the Seacat anti-aircraft missile launcher on board HMS *Cavalier* in Brighton Marina. *Author*

Below:
HMS *Alliance* at the Royal Navy Submarine Museum, Gosport on 8 August 1984. *Author*

Below:
HMS *Stickleback*, an Imperial War Museum exhibit at Duxford airfield. Beside her is a Japanese Long Lance torpedo of World War 2. *Author*

midget submarine (similar to *X24* at Gosport) she is larger than one expects. Nevertheless her interior is too cramped for public access, so she can only be viewed from outside. Part of the wreckage from an operational wartime X-craft can also be seen at Duxford, together with a variety of other large naval exhibits. These include torpedoes, guns, the bulk of the Imperial War Museum's ship model collection and a number of Fleet Air Arm aircraft. There is also a submarine-launched Polaris missile — a dummy practice one. Compressed air blasts the missile to the surface where a solid fuel rocket motor takes over.

Open: *17 March-4 November:* Daily 11.00-17.30 (16.45 from 21 October).
Closed: Good Friday; May Day; all winter.
Admission: (to whole public area of complex) £1.50p Adults; 80p Children and OAPs.
Facilities for disabled: Fully accessible.

Cornwall Aero Park and Flambards Village

Culdrose, Cornwall. Tel (03265)-3404/4549. On the A3083 between Helston and Culdrose.

An all-weather family leisure park set in beautiful landscaped gardens. Indoor exhibitions include Flambards Victorian Village, 'Britain in the Blitz' and many historic aircraft. Because of its proximity to HMS *Seahawk* (the Royal Naval Air Station at Culdrose), there is particular emphasis on helicopters and their employment in the Falklands campaign. This is enlivened by a computerised audio-visual display. There is also a major exhibition on air-sea rescue in the southwest.

Open: *Easter-October:* Daily 10.00-17.00.
Closed: Winter.
Admission: £2.20p Adults; £1.00 Children.
Facilities for disabled: Suitably accessible.

Broadlands

Romsey, Hamsphire. Tel (0794)-516878. Off the Romsey bypass.

The career of Admiral of the Fleet Earl Mountbatten of Burma spans the history of the Royal Navy in the 20th century. He was born in 1900, great-grandson of Queen Victoria. His father, Prince Louis of Battenberg, was a serving officer in the Royal Navy and was first Sea Lord on the outbreak of World War 1 in 1914. Lord Louis himself joined the Navy in 1913 and served in HMS *Lion* and HMS *Queen Elizabeth*, Admiral Beatty's flagships of the Battlecruiser Fleet and the Grand Fleet. He also spent some time in patrol craft and in one of the 'K' class steam-driven submarines. By the end of World War 1 anti-German hysteria had forced the Battenbergs to change their family name to Mountbatten, while their Russian relatives (Tsar Nicholas II and his family) had been murdered by revolutionaries.

Lord Louis's postwar study at University was followed by two Empire tours as Flag-Lieutenant to his cousin the Prince of Wales (later King Edward

VIII). In 1922 Lord Louis married Edwina Ashley, who was later to inherit Broadlands. This house had once been the home of Lord Palmerston, the Prime Minister whose imperial and naval policies were so much a feature of Queen Victoria's reign.

Specialising in wireless communications, Lord Louis subsequently commanded the destroyers *Daring* and *Wishart*. At the Naval Air Division of the Admiralty, he was involved in the integration of the Fleet Air Arm into the Royal Navy, and he also advocated the introduction of the Swiss-designed Oerlikon 20mm gun. His most famous ship was the flotilla-leader *Kelly*, whose short but action-packed career ended under dive-bombing off Crete. Lord Louis then headed Combined Operations Command, and became C-in-C South-East Asia Command, which culminated in the ceremonial Japanese surrender at Singapore.

In March 1947 Lord Louis arrived in Delhi as Viceroy to oversee the transfer of independence to India and Pakistan: and when that occurred on 14/15 August 1947, the last Viceroy became the first Governor-General of India. It was not until 1948 that he returned to seagoing service. Command of a cruiser squadron was eventually followed by the post of C-in-C Mediterranean. In 1955 he became First Sea Lord, being largely responsible for the organisation of the unified Ministry of Defence which was undertaken in 1964. Lady Edwina Mountbatten had died in 1960, and in 1979 Lord Mountbatten's own active retirement ended when he was murdered by an IRA bomb. He lies in Romsey Abbey.

The life and times of Lord Mountbatten are portrayed in full in exhibit and photograph, splendid uniform and technical relic, document and audio-visual display. The house and grounds of Broadlands itself are also open to the public.

By birth and achievement, Lord Mountbatten's career was unique. And yet, at the same time, it is typical of service in the Royal Navy. For every successful naval man must be at home in both the ceremonial and the mundane; he must be able to assimilate complicated information without becoming bogged down in unnecessary detail; he must be able to assume responsibility, yet delegate, inspire loyalty and affection without forfeiting respect or jeopardising discipline; he must switch from being in sole command of ship or unit, to being a junior member of a team, and back again; to transfer from office work to ship-handling to technical study; he must co-operate with civil authorities, other forces, other nationalities, and even yesterday's enemy.

All those things are of everyday occurrence in the Royal Navy.

Open: *April-July:* Tuesdays-Sundays and Bank Holiday Mondays 10.00-17.00; *August-September:* Daily 10.00-17.00.
Closed: Mondays in April-July (except Bank Holiday Mondays); all winter.
Admission: £2.40 Adults; £1.70 OAPs, Students and Disabled; £1.20 Children; £6 Family Ticket (two adults plus three children).
Facilities for disabled: Grounds and Ground Floor accessible only.
Nearest station: Romsey.

The Hidden Royal Navy

You expect to see warships — operational or preserved, abandoned or being used as houseboats — at the seaside. Nor is it surprising that most local museums on the coast feature shipwrecks, a naval hero born, or some vessel built in the area. Metallurgy, radar and aeronautics are but three of many technological processes of naval significance and nationwide production, any one of which can be encountered in displays of scientific or industrial archaeology. But, in addition to all these aspects, the Navy can be seen almost anywhere. For example, Rockingham Castle near Market Harborough contains a number of exhibits relating to the careers of the Seymours, Culme-Seymours and Watsons, who have served in the Navy from the reign of Henry VIII to the present day. Jane Austen's House at Chawton in Hampshire, has a display devoted to her brothers serving in the Royal Navy. Admiral-of-the-Fleet Sir Francis Austen (1774-1865) was C-in-C of the North American and West Indies station, while Rear-Admiral Charles Austen (1779-1852) was C-in-C East Indies. Regimental museums often have maritime associations, frequently because their forebears served as marines in some naval battle. The ship's badge and detailed history of the fast minelayer HMS *Abdiel* can be seen at Airborne Forces Museum in Aldershot — on 10 September 1943, she had just arrived at Taranto carrying 400 paratroops when she detonated a magnetic mine and sank with very heavy loss of life.

Ships' crests can be used as a variety of ornaments or decoration. They are often to be found in museums or churches of towns which adopted a wartime vessel during the National Savings Warship Week of 14-21 February 1942.

Some associations have continued to the present day, a warship adopting a local children's hospital or other charitable organisation (perhaps itself of naval foundation). Officers and ratings help with projects and fetes, providing toys and presents for overseas. Inevitably the local hostelry acquires the ship's crest for display in the bar. There may be a photograph of the ship, which perhaps grows into a miniature exhibition of naval history. Practically every ship engaged in the Falklands campaign is portrayed in the bar of the Lord Leycester Hotel in Warwick.

Inn signs are a fruitful source of maritime interest. Heroes, battles and warships are all commemorated. Most are located near dockyards, but they can be seen anywhere in the country. So, too, can street names with naval association. Trafalgar Square is probably the most famous of such examples, its layout dominated by Nelson's Column.

No part of the country is without some commemoration of a naval hero, or memorial to the missing at sea, or the grave of someone whose body was recovered or of someone who survived to die peacefully at home far from the dangers of the sea and the violence of the enemy. These remembrancers range from the massive divisional memorials at Portsmouth, Plymouth and Chatham to neat flower-trimmed graves, from noble statues to a fading single-line dedication on a crumbling headstone in an overgrown and long-forgotten churchyard.

Top:
The distinctive hull lines of this Portchester houseboat show that it was once a British Power Boat Co MGB. *Author*

Above:
Rockingham Castle in Leicestershire may be far from the sea, but its exhibits include personal trophies and memorabilia of many generations of sailors who have lived there.
Cdr L. M. M. Saunders Watson

Above:
Jane Austen's House at Chawton in Hampshire may seem an unlikely place to see items of Royal Navy history, but two of the novelist's brothers were admirals, and part of the display describes their careers. *Author*

Right:
The surviving buildings of what was once the Royal Victoria Victualling Yard in Deptford (1742-1869) have been converted into flats and community premises. *Author*

Below right:
Looking towards Nelson's Column in Trafalgar Square from Whitehall, on 12 May 1984. *Author*

Below:
Taranto Hill at Yeovilton in Somerset. *Author*

Above:
The Nelson, Yeovil, Somerset. *Author*

Right:
The Wyvern, Lee-on-Solent,
Hampshire. Note the Westland
Dragonfly helicopter in the
background on the sign. *Author*

Below:
Alton Cemetery, Hampshire. *Author*

Insignia: RN Officers

Cap Badge

Beret Badge

Flag Officers

Commodore, Captain & Commander

FLAG OFFICERS' SLEEVE LACE AND SHOULDER BADGES

FLAG OFFICERS' SHOULDER STRAPS

Admiral of the Fleet

Admiral

Vice-Admiral

Rear-Admiral

Admiral of the Fleet

Admiral

Vice Admiral

Rear Admiral

OTHER OFFICERS' SLEEVE LACE, SHOULDER STRAPS AND SHOULDER BADGES

Commodore

Captain

Commander

Lieut.-Commander

Lieutenant

Sub-Lieutenant

Midshipman (lapel)

Insignia: RN Ratings

Supply and Secretariat

Radio Operator (General)

Radio Operator (Tactical)

Tactical Systems (Submarines)

Electronic Warfare

Commando

Subsunk Parachute Assistance Group

Radar

Sonar

Seaman

RATE BADGES

SHOULDER BADGES

Fleet Chief Petty Officer (Warrant Officer)

Chief Petty Officer (Buttons on cuff)

Petty Officer

Leading Rate

Fleet Chief Petty Officer (Warrant Officer)

Chief Petty Officer

144